MAN
HIS WORLD
AND
HIS WORK

MAN

HIS WORLD
AND
HIS WORK

Louis M. Savary, (S.J.)

PAULIST PRESS EXPLORATION BOOKS

NEW YORK   GLEN ROCK   WESTMINSTER

AMSTERDAM   TORONTO

Facultas Edendi:
Edward J. Sponga, S.J.
Provincial, Maryland Prov.
November 22, 1966
Nihil Obstat:
William F. Hogan, S.T.D.
Censor Librorum
Imprimatur:
Thomas A. Boland, S.T.D.
Archbishop of Newark
January 6, 1967

Published by Paulist Press
Editorial Office: 304 W. 58th St., N. Y., N. Y. 10019
Business Office: Glen Rock, New Jersey 07452
Printed and bound in the
United States of America

ACKNOWLEDGMENTS

McGraw-Hill Book Company: "Industry and the Family" from *Industrial Sociology* by Eugene V. Schneider. Copyright © 1957 McGraw-Hill, Inc. Used by permission of McGraw-Hill Book Company.

"The Individual and the Group at Work in Contemporary Society" by A. G. Brown, S.J. and "Aging and Retirement in Contemporary Society" by Paula Zelipsky. Printed by permission of A. G. Brown, S.J.

E. M. Standing: "The Work of the Child" from *Maria Montessori: Her Life and Work,* pp. 141-158. Copyright © 1962 by E. Mortimer Standing. Reprinted with permission.

James W. Trent, Irene J. Athey and Judith L. Craise, "Technology, Education and Human Development," *The Educational Record* 46 (Spring, 1965), pp. 93-103. Reprinted with permission of American Council on Education, Washington, D.C.

Cora Du Bois, "The Dominant Value Profile of American Culture," *American Anthropologist* 57 (1955), pp. 1232-1239. Reprinted with permission.

Robert L. Heilbroner, "Men and Machines in Perspective," *The Public Interest* (Fall, 1965), pp. 27-36. Reprinted with permission from Basic Books, Inc.

Helen Rowan, "The Creative People: How to Spot Them," reprinted by permission from THINK Magazine, published by IBM, copyright © 1962 by International Business Machines Corporation.

Joseph Thomas, "Une théologie du travail?" reprinted in English (translation by Sr. Mary Nicholas, R.S.M.) with permission of *Projet: Revue de l'action populaire* 164 (January, 1963), pp. 5-18; "Perspectives sur une théologie du travail," reprinted in English (translation by Sr. Mary Nicholas, R.S.M.) with permission of *Projet: Revue de l'action populaire* 166 (March, 1963), pp. 260-272.

Harper & Row Publishers Incorporated: *Teilhard de Chardin and the Mystery of Christ* by Christopher F. Mooney, p. 205. Copyright © 1966 by Christopher F. Mooney. *The Divine Milieu* by Teilhard de Chardin, p. 19. English translation copyright © 1960 by William Collins Sons & Co., Ltd., London, and Harper & Row, Publishers, Incorporated, New York. Reprinted by permission of Harper & Row, Publishers, Inc.

The Macmillan Company: *The Secular City* by Harvey Cox, p. 189. Copyright © 1965 by Harvey Cox.

Doubleday & Company, Inc.: From *Irrational Man,* by William Barrett, pp. 24-25. Copyright © 1958 by William Barrett. Reprinted by permission of Doubleday & Company, Inc.

P. J. Kenedy & Sons: "A Believer's Look at the World," by Johannes B. Metz in *The Christian and the World: Readings in Theology,* excerpts from pp. 71-89. Copyright © 1965.

CONTENTS

v

I
AN EXPERIMENT IN
THEOLOGICAL REFLECTION

Most Americans live their lives in a world of intense productive activity. This human effort is carried on in the quiet of a library, in a biology laboratory, at an architect's desk; or it takes place in a noisy automobile factory, a steel mill, a newspaper office. From the housewife to the board of bank directors, from the grocery boy to the astronaut, one experience universally shared is *work*. Work is at the center and focus of life: personal life, family life, the community, the nation, the world. Our whole existence seems more than ever before in history to revolve around action, production, efficiency, automation, technology, employment. Man works at his job, he works at home, and in America he even "works" at his recreation. His mind is preoccupied with work that "must be done" either by himself or others. A man's career is his work. In describing himself to another, an individual will sum up his past life and his present concern by telling his inquirer where he has been employed and what his educational preparation has been; he will mention his present occupational status, and the levels of job advancement he hopes to achieve in the future. The world of work, then, is central to life for the contemporary American.

The question posed to the Christian committed to Christ is simply this: What is the meaning of work in my Christian life? The task of answering this question belongs fundamentally to each Christian, it is his personal responsibility.

The goal of this book is to point out a fresh and experimental pathway of theological reflection to enable the individual Christian to answer the question of the meaning of work in his Christian life. This approach is both experimental and personal.

It is an *experimental* approach in the sense that we shall make our theological reflections upon the data offered by the social sciences regarding work. Human work has a different meaning for a psychologist, a sociologist, an anthropologist, an economist. For example, for the psychologist work can be simply a setting for motivational studies, while the educator may see work as a set of careers for which he must adequately prepare his students. We shall look at the various meanings given to work by the different academic disciplines and try to re-understand those human meanings and their implications in order to arrive at a fuller Christian meaning of work.

The theological method we follow is also *personal*. We do not propose in these pages to give *the* meaning of work for the Christian in his world of work. Rather, we simply hope to bring to light ideas, insights, and dimensions from which a Christian might find for himself a deeper human and divine meaning in his life through his work.

Hence, the method of reflection on the findings of the social scientists which we shall employ chapter by chapter differs from the most common traditional method of theological reflection. Such a traditional analysis would use as matter for its reflection the data of Christian revelation regarding work, as (1) found in scripture and the documents of the Church, (2) seen within the philosophical setting of the essential nature of man. In this approach the meaning of work for the Christian would seem to be "absolutely" discoverable through an analysis of these two sources of information. That is, work would have a Christian meaning which would be independent of the individual personality, history and scientific achievement.

However, in searching for the matter for such a traditional reflection, Peter Schoonenberg in *God's World in the Making* remarks that we simply have insufficient data in the sources of revelation to construct a Christian ethos of labor—one that goes beyond incidental admonition to discover the role and meaning of work in human life. In the face of this inadequacy in the sources of revelation we are forced, happily perhaps, to experiment creatively with other source material for theological reflection on the problem of work.

Such experimentation is encouraged by Vatican II. In fact, it would seem that regarding the problem of work in the Christian's life, the Church itself recognizes the number and importance of the human elements in the problem of work which must be faced, understood and integrated into a historical perspective of the Christian's viewpoint toward work in this age of "unremitting secularity." In section 54 of Vatican's II's pastoral constitution on "The Church in the Modern World" we read:

> The circumstances of the life of modern man have been so profoundly changed in their social and cultural aspect, that we can speak of a new age of human history. New ways are open, therefore, for the perfection and the further extension of culture. These ways have been prepared by the enormous growth of natural, human and social sciences, by technical progress, and advances in developing and organizing means whereby men can communicate with one another. Hence the culture of today possesses particular characteristics: sciences which are called exact greatly develop critical judgment; the more recent psychological studies more profoundly explain human activity; historical studies make it much easier to see things in their mutable and evolutionary aspects; customs and usages are becoming more and more uniform; industrialization, urbanization and other causes which promote community living create a mass-culture from which are born new ways of thinking, acting and making use of leisure.

It must be noted that although our program is basically one of method (theological reflection upon the findings of the social scientists regarding the human meaning of work), the goal of the book is not merely to give the reader practice in using a new and different method of theological reflection. Much more especially, the intent here is to present material for the analysis of the Christian so that through such reflection he might discover the complicated richness of meaning for his Christian life offered by the daily work of his life.

Work and the Social Sciences and Theology

To paint in broad lines the directions this book will take we present here a quick survey of the place of work in each of the social sciences and other disciplines as represented by the selections in the following chapters. This will be followed by a glimpse of work in the contemporary Christian's life as seen in some approaches to a theology of work.

The *sociologist's* interest in work is unquestioned. He is interested in groups of people: the family, the work team, social and political organizations and many more. At home in the power structures of political and social movements, the sociologist finds that work and occupations are a fundamental source of motivational forces there, because of unemployment, social security, discrimination, and the quest for power. Eugene V. Schneider analyzes the strong interrelation between industry and family. Paula Zelipsky, in another selection, studies the effects of modern technology upon the retired worker.

From the time of Dewey and the pragmatists the overriding purpose of *education* has been to prepare the student for life. People such as Maria Montessori have been deeply concerned with the meaning of the child's "work" in his growth and development. Fundamental to the educator's view of life in society is an understanding of man as a productive element in the community. Hence education is often for a career or a job and concerns itself with the person's intellectual and physical aptitude for specific life-vocations. James W. Trent and his associates statistically study the changing pattern of the undergraduate school in the light of the vocational and other interests of the students. For, connected very intimately with a man's occupation or work are the questions of prestige, security, family, amount of education, salary, and all the other variables in the career-function facing each student and his counselor.

In the *anthropologist's* area of concern, work is a pivotal element. Work influences and is influenced by family, culture, role, status, education, religion, politics, technology, geography, art and recreation. According to Cora Du Bois' "Profile of American Cultural Values," work is one of the three focal cultural values which she feels are the keys to the development and understanding of the history and present status of American culture.

Work is a preoccupying, though often unnoticed, interest of *psychology*. The deep influences of work as a reflection of cultural values in American living make it important in the development of personality. The extreme age groups, children and old people, studied in the earlier chapters, are used to explore the phenomenon of work, the better to reflect and isolate the basic nature of man, his self-understanding and meaning. Work situations offer many of the best experimental set-ups for studying group dynamics, decision making, the psychological factors of motivation and emotional health. A. G. Brown, S.J., a social psychologist, looks at work through the eyes of the corporation and surveys some of the psychological procedures employed by the organization to improve productive efficiency.

The *economist* and his approach to things presupposes the fundamental and all-embracing importance of work. Production, supply and demand, budgets, inflation, poverty, employment and many other faces appear in the world of man's work. Robert L. Heilbroner tries to assess the economic effects of automation, which is gradually rendering human effort itself "redundant."

Helen Rowan tells us that the *business analyst* sees the creative person as essentially necessary to the life and growth of the corporation. From another aspect of creativity, the *artist* today is faced with the problem of revitalizing the meaning of the object in our present-day "dispensable" and "throw-away" world.

The *Christian philosopher* is concerned with work because it makes him face squarely the problem of the meaning of man and his relation to the material world. He must discuss the problem of the nature of work itself, its dignity, its necessity, its desirability. What in man's life is the function of aesthetic and artistic creativity, of leisure and recreation, of contemplation and reflection? W. Norris Clarke, S.J., surveys the many possibilities of "creative leisure" open to today's worker.

In this way, then, is the stage set for a study of the formal theological treatment of work. For the *theologian* and for Christian man and his spirituality, work makes us search for a solution to the basic question posed by the penitential, creationist, and eschatological approaches to the life of grace here on earth. If the Christian must take a risk, is it better to plunge into the work of harnessing the universe and following secular man in his dedication to technology and the future and to risk forgetting God? Or is it better to concentrate on the heavenly kingdom in contemplation and prayer, avoiding the infection of the secular and thereby risking the loss of contact with the vital and vigorous forces of energy and love of an earthful of human minds and hearts?

Both the atheist and the Christian agree on the profound significance of the world and man's work in it. The real question is concerned with the relevance of the world and man's work for the community of persons and the "permanent persons," the continuing community of man. Whom is work for? Why do we have it? Where does it lead? For Joseph Thomas, Christ is the center of a Christian theology of work and he studies the importance of the growth of the body of Christ and the sacramental sources of its life. With the help of ideas from Johannes B. Metz and Christopher Mooney, we consider the necessity of an approach to the world as non-Godly, as distinct from God, in order to honestly approach a theological meaning of the world and man's work.

In order to begin to answer the problem of the meaning of work for the Christian on the theological level, we must take into consideration the facts of the case as presented not only by scriptural and theological teachings but also by the conclusions and findings which years of labor in the social sciences have brought to light concerning man and his world and how he makes his way in it.

Dialogue with the Social Sciences

Our method of relating the social sciences to theology is in no sense some new radical innovation in theology. Rather our method should be viewed within the context of a manifest attempt in our day to encourage real dialogue between the social scientist and the theologian. For, in fact, comparatively little dialogue went on in the past between theology and the fields of psychology, anthropology, sociology, and economics. More recently, although there has no longer been general and open enmity and suspicion when theologians and social scientists meet one another, much of what has transpired has not been dialogue in any genuine sense.

Yet there is widespread interest in such dialogue. This is shown by programs like that of the Academy of Religion and Mental Health, and books such as *The Nature of Man in Theological and Psychological Perspective,* edited by Simon Doniger. It is perhaps also true to say that the theologians have displayed more interest in the discoveries of the cultural and psychological disciplines than the social scientist in the reflections and insights of religious thinkers.

We must recognize that experts in each field have various opinions about their views of man. Among theologians also there are some disagreements about man, his nature, the working of grace, creation. One particularly touchy controversy among Christian theologians today is about *method.* No one denies the importance of the findings of psychology, sociology and the other behavioral sciences, but the point at issue is the meaning these sciences have for theology. Positions like Karl Barth's regard the conclusions of social and cultural disciplines as purely preliminary. Others like Reinhold Niebuhr believe that such knowledge, even though it bears only an external relation to theology, is important and should be studied. Tillich goes beyond Barth and Niebuhr and says that no relevant modern theology can deny the contributions of the behavioral disciplines, that this knowledge affects theologizing internally as well as externally, for it affects man's "existence" although not his "essence." Seward Hiltner of Princeton Theological Seminary takes the last step and holds that there is a "psychology" that is a proper branch of theology, internal to theology itself, hence, "as potentially revelatory of man's 'essence' as any other branch of theology." [1]

To preserve a proper balance here, it should be pointed out that there is also a proper branch of each social science that is

---

[1] S. Hiltner, "Conclusion: The Dialogue on Man's Nature," in Simon Doniger, ed., *The Nature of Man in Theological and Psychological Perspective* (New York: Harper, 1962), p. 254.

concerned with "religion." The religion and culture of a society cannot be studied independently of its economic dimension and social context. Furthermore, says Harvey Cox in *The Secular City* (New York: Macmillan, 1965), religion "is imbedded in behavior and institutions before it is consciously codified, and the alteration of social economic patterns always entails religious change" (p. 8). For example, the theologian speaks of sin, the psychologist of guilt. The two concepts are deeply related and yet each notion was developed within the rules, elements and methods of separate disciplines. It is not an easy matter for the theologian to grasp what the psychologist means by the term "guilt," nor for the scientist to comprehend the theological meaning of sin.

The problem of the double discipline approach is a bit more subtle regarding work. For the term work is employed by each of the social sciences as well as philosophy and theology, often without being clearly defined. At most each discipline gives work a meaning proper to its own context and interest.

This study acknowledges in human work the existence of basic relations between the social sciences and theology. The majority of the selections in the study present some findings on the meaning of work in sociology, psychology, anthropology, education and economics. The articles are for the most part summary articles, surveying the facts and implications of human work as seen from the viewpoints of the various sciences. The last part of the study looks at work more philosophically and theologically.

The synthesis called for must be made by the theologian in his life, by the social scientist in his, and by each Christian insofar as this is possible. In this last case, the dialogue envisioned is one between the Christian who is practically and behaviorally trying to integrate his total life, especially his work-life, into his Christ-life, and the more speculative conclusions of the disciplines of social science, philosophy and theology. Hopefully, the Christian will be able to see more fully and more deeply the social, psychological, cultural, rational, human and divine forces influencing his life and work.

Perspectives for an Approach to the Question

In order to place our theological reflections in a proper context throughout the following chapters, we will do well before we begin the formal work to discuss summarily three important facets of the problem of the Christian in his world of work: (1) the complexity of the meaning of work; (2) the effects of secularization and technology upon contemporary man; and (3) the specifically personal character of the meaning and definition that work will have for each individual.

1. *The Complexity of the Meaning of Work*

To be a human today is difficult enough. To be asked what it means today to be a Christian in the world of work is often embarrassing. For the answer to this question demands that the Christian explain how he can genuinely be at the same time a citizen of two cities, human and divine. The committed Christian who is deeply involved in the progress of the secular city is faced with the problem of integrating his double vocation. The complexity of contemporary human life alone is overwhelming; the complexity of an integral Christian life is staggering. But if the question is to be faced, and if at least the elements of a solution are to be discovered, we must explore the Christian facing his work and his accomplishments in the city of man. Human work lies at the intersection where man confronts creation. Here, in that spending of human effort which each man calls his work, is the locus of man's productive self-expression and a place where we can begin to search for an understanding of today's Christian.

If we accept the premise concerning the centrality of the findings of the social sciences in our theological reflection, it immediately follows that the findings of social science add to the complexity of the meaning of Christian work; furthermore, the number of elements and dimensions of human effort which enter into the problem as well as the relative importance of each of these to the Christian and his work are variables subject to the process of history.

A job is an essential ingredient of every life given to God; one must pay his bills in order to live in society and must live there in order to serve God there. Such is the minimal meaning of their daily work for many American Christians. We are all aware of clergymen who in good faith have romanticized the layman's occupations "so that they could actually believe that a man could adequately serve God through his plumbing or his engineering." And "the laity have not objected," says a Protestant layman at an inter-faith discussion, "for this was an easy way out. 'Do a good job,' 'Be a good professional'—that was your bounden duty to God, on a par with 'proclaiming' the Word. I do research in the chemistry of metals; the minister preaches and counsels; thus we both serve God through our work. Rot! . . . It is sheer nonsense to claim that because a man has done his work well, i.e., has built up a successful business, become an eminent scientist or a master of the Grange, he has fulfilled God's calling.[2]

What is the relation between being a Christian and being a citizen of the secular city? Certainly, God's calling an individual to be a committed Christian implies that the individual has an obligation to do his job well. But when this drive to success is confusedly equated with fulfilling God's will, the job is painlessly idolized. This attitude is not only erroneous but naive. There are many other Christian values involved in our work of which every Christian should be acutely aware. For example, every Christian must learn to see his job as a participation in the ecumenical strategy of the Church, as a member of a body which has accepted a collective responsibility for all of creation.

In addition to the specifically Christian dimensions of work, the findings of social science add their discoveries of unconscious motivations, social and cultural pressures, economic forces and educational needs to complicate the matter.

"Our world is almost totally different from the ideas being used to describe it," says David Bazelon in *The Paper Economy*. Each science has its own image of man. There is a new world forming before our eyes. A man cannot have his eyes open for very long before he realizes how different things are in the world today. There is

---

[2] "The Layman's Vocation in the World, A Protestant View," *Newsletter of the Matthew Ricci Academy* (December 1964), p. 4.

for instance a new rapidity in the way styles go out of style. A teen-
agers' hit song is old after a month. An automobile even a few years
old is obsolete. New synthetic fabrics are invented daily. The creativity in all the physical and social sciences and in our space program is enormous. The levels of existence discovered and explored
by psychiatrists, parapsychologists, artists—on the levels of consciousness, unconsciousness, subconsciousness, preconsciousness,
superconsciousness—are all new. The developing study of peripheral
knowledge forms in, for example, *The Silent Language* and *The
Hidden Dimension* (both written by Edward T. Hall) brings man
through cultural anthropological studies into higher degrees of understanding and unity. The human phenomenon, says Teilhard, is
essentially defined by the development of human thought. Empirical,
analytic, reflective studies carry whole fields of knowledge cascad-
ing into libraries and journals. They deepen man's understanding of
himself, asking more questions than can be solved. Mankind is moving with passion.

2. *The Effects of Secularization and Technology*

The rise of urban civilization and the apotheosis of technology
are not the only characteristics of our day. The decline of religion
is another, and this decline is not merely an intellectual loss of interest in theological speculation; it is more concrete and deep. In the
words of William Barrett in *Irrational Man* (Garden City: Doubleday, 1962), "religion is no longer the uncontested center and ruler
of man's life . . . the Church is no longer the final and unquestioned
home and asylum of his being" (p. 24). This waning of religion did
not happen overnight. It began many centuries ago, but the complete
realization of the meaning of this decline has only come upon us
recently. Barrett summarizes the *homelessness* of man as a result of
the decline.

> The loss of the Church was the loss of a whole system of sym-
> bols, images, dogmas, and rites which had the psychological
> validity of immediate experience, and within which hitherto
> the whole psychic life of Western man had been safely con-

tained. In losing religion, man lost the concrete connection with a transcendent realm of being; he was set free to deal with the world in all its brute objectivity. But he was bound to feel homeless in such a world, which no longer answered the needs of his spirit (p. 25).

A home is a "psychic container" of our life. To be homeless means to become a wanderer. The Church in its sacramental life had given man the possibility of human completeness. The Church introduced and explained to man the meaning of creation and community as well as his relationship to God. With the decline of religion man became alienated from all these: man became a stranger to God, to nature and to the entire social structure. The worst and final step in the alienation process, as the existential philosophers see it, is the inevitable consequence of the previous alienations: man's alienation from his own self.

Nevertheless, though our era is one where religion is conspicuously absent, the forces of secularism are not fanatically anti-religious. In fact, they show no interest in persecuting religion; secularism merely passes religion by and focuses its interest on other things. As secularism spreads throughout the globe, fewer and fewer look to institutional religion for a comprehensive system of personal and cosmic meaning.

If today's world is a different world from yesterday's, then in the world context work (human effort) takes on new meanings. With the decline of "religion," the secular meaning of work is emphasized, evolution and progress are the keynotes.

The evolution and progress provided by technology is not slight, especially in regard to human work. We no longer have a world of slave labor; we no longer are a country where indentured servants are common. We no longer have a country without child labor laws or with inhumanly long working days. We no longer normally have sweat shops and unhealthy working conditions. We are no longer without social security and fair employment practices. Our attitudes toward education, toward children, toward the aged, toward women, all have been modified. The assembly line is as common as nylon. The symbol of mass production in the 1960's is the plastic bag. Communication improvements have reduced the size of the earth to a neighborhood, while it has enlarged the world of our relationships and responsibilities to an unbelievable complexity. Automation, transistors, synthetic fabrics, Xerox, computers, and all the other hallmarks of our day have reworked our world so that a person who passed his last days on earth only ten years ago would find it incredible were he to be resurrected today.

Despite the existence of TV dinners, people still go to bed hungry. Though there are scores of colleges and universities across the country, there are still many uneducated people standing on street corners. Nevertheless many in America have wants that are very different from those of the rest of the world. If the majority of people in the world have fundamental need of food, warmth, clothing and shelter, these elements of life are taken for granted in America. Today the American's felt needs are for *security* and *status*. People in the United States want to get ahead, to get higher degrees, to get better jobs, live in better homes. The adjectives of the admen are always comparative—more, better, quicker, higher—and superlative. Where some nations seek simply food, we in America seek *better* food or the *best* food. This cultural need of the comparative and the superlative has its influence in our employments and occupations.

If we agree that, in general in America, work no longer implies the urgency of subsistence, we also admit the growing complexity of social organization and the consequent introduction of a number of social ailments. These ailments often find their source in the existing alienation between the individual and the groups of which an American is a member, founded on the disparity between the official ideology and ideals of society on the one hand, and the actualities of daily living as a working citizen on the other. *Anomie* is the word coined by Emile Durkheim to signify the experience felt by the individual who lacks goals and guideposts in his life. The word is used to describe the condition of the individual who has high ideals and a lively sense of ethics but who is forced in his everyday life to compromise these ideals and values.

With the concrete problems we face in the fields of labor and employment, poverty and migration, politics and retirement, we see the overwhelming complexity of our networks of human relationships. If the "theoretical" elements of the problem of work are difficult enough to integrate, how can we ever begin to fit into meaningfulness the paradox of growth and decay, of abundance and poverty, of altruism and selfishness, which exist side by side and which cannot be avoided or dismissed?

Man has a deep desire to "grasp the handle," to catch a glimpse of the "big picture," to see where the world is moving. As Christians we believe that the whole of creation is moving toward Christ and we seek to discover the manner in which this development is to occur. How does the creator see the "big picture"? How can we come to get a glimpse of it, to receive adequate motivation and direction and purpose in our confrontation with other men and the material world? The total painting is made up of many brush strokes and each stroke is a living and working and loving human being. Always, we are faced with a double question: that of the individual Christian and his problems in confronting matter through work; and that of the communal problem of mankind on its journey to the *eschaton* —the meaning of the growth of the mystical body and the place of material creation in the divine plan. The complex of elements that go to make up the problem of work must be understood in both contexts, the individual and the collective. The problems are not the same in the two spheres. Nor are the answers, the meanings to be found for the expenditure of human energy.

3.　*The Personal Definition of Work*

As we saw earlier, the definition of work depends entirely upon one's viewpoint. For the economist, work is labor, a variable factor in the production function. For the psychologist work is a setting for studying motivation, emotions, decision-making, interpersonal relationships. For the anthropologist work is a dimension of culture. For the artist work is creativity. For the educator work is the career for which he must prepare his students. For the sociologist work is a focal point for group dynamics, social structure and status. Each philosopher sees in work a different meaning: For Marx work is the essence of life, for Dewey work is that in and through which man expresses his desire to live in cooperative friendship with others, for some neo-Aristotelians work is the servant of leisure. For the theologian work is that activity wherein man confronts material creation.

Work in the bible includes everything from the activity of God in creation to the toil of a slave. Work for the millionaire means worry, decisions involving mountains of money and multitudes of people, total preoccupation. For the lonely spinster work is what makes the days pass just a bit faster. To a housewife work often means only drudgery. To the retired man sitting on a park bench work is a memory.

To the student work is study, to the unemployed work is survival, to the teenager tired of school work means a job, and a job means freedom and independence. The "work" of the child is becoming, growing. Work means something different to a newspaper boy, an astronaut, a hatcheck girl, a plumber, a congressman, a writer, a musician, a doctor, a nuclear physicist, a psychiatrist, a priest.

The economic, psychological and cultural dimensions which enter into each man's concept of work are many. The purpose of this book is not to constrict in any way the meanings which work can have, but to remain open to whatever appears on whatever level it appears. Let the migrant worker and the millionaire both speak what they see. Let all who are citizens of both cities strive to discharge their earthly duties in response to the spirit of the gospel.

It is the gift of faith which allows a man to see the interpenetration of his *secular vocation* and *divine calling,* between his secular work and his Christian work. It is in the fundamentally Christian context of the life which is divine love which drives us to unify our two vocations, somehow to blend heaven and earth, to participate in the construction of the new earth whose blueprints are seen clearly only to God. It is in man's productive efforts upon material creation where the divine calling and the secular vocation unite.

As Christ is the principle and agent of creation, he is also the healer of creation. To accomplish the latter, Christ, the radiance of the Father, brought new being and new power, new light and new warmth into God's darkling but dawning world, radically transforming it. It is in this same world where men cooperate with Christ in rebuilding the body of man and in fulfilling creation. Here, where man and creation meet, where the two vocations are united, lies the problem of the meaning of work for the Christian.

Questions for Discussion

1. In what sense is this approach to theological reflection experimental? In what sense is it personal?
2. How does this approach differ from the most common traditional method?
3. How is work seen by each of the various disciplines here?
4. What differences of method do we find in present-day efforts at dialogue between theologians and social scientists?
5. What are the three facets of the problem of the Christian in his world of work? Discuss.

II
WORK AND THE FAMILY

A. Prenote

The family is a physiological, psychological, social, cultural, legal, educational, economic and religious unit. Hence, not surprisingly, the family is a focal point for practically every social, behavioral and biological science. Just as the family is the undisputed nucleus for the development of the human personality, so too today religious educationalists acknowledge the family as the center for the development of the Christian life.

The family both as a unit and in its individual members is related to work in many ways. In this chapter we look at the family and its members through the eyes of the sociologist. Eugene V. Schneider points out in his essay the many radical changes in the meaning and function of the family which have come about with the rise of technology and industry: the growing "importance" of the child, the emerging equality of various family roles, the disappearance of the extended family.

From the few facts adduced in Schneider's article alone we can conclude that the radical sociological changes in family structure and meaning which are the results of changes in the industrial world will have their effect on the family as source of Christian thought and behavior.

Since it is not yet a common practice to offer for theological reflection an article from a sociologist's pen, we must learn to read such works with a new mentality. Besides reading with our eyes open for facts, we must remember that our theological reflection calls for a Christian attitude of loving concern for that created world which God gave to man to know and control.

Perhaps the speculative theologian would object at the outset that what we propose to do here is not at all "theological reflection." Perhaps not. Whatever we wish to call our activity, it is at root "Christian reflection": an attempt on the part of one who is committed to Christ and his Church to know and understand more deeply God's gift of life and creation and to use all available powers, potential and knowledge to more clearly and consciously serve him in love.

The following selection is taken from pp. 425-433 of *Industrial Sociology* (New York: McGraw-Hill, 1957). In keeping with the nature of the present book, certain purely scholarly footnotes are omitted.

B. Selection: Industry and the Family

Here we shall consider the way in which industry and the family are related in our society. For reasons that have already been discussed, the family must be considered the oldest and probably most important of human groups. It is within the family that man has his most significant educational, emotional, affectional, and sexual experiences. The family is the most vulnerable and most easily modified of all institutions, and at the same time one of the toughest. It bows before all the passing winds of fortune; it is easily crushed by physiological, social and economic changes. And, yet, in one form or another, it always survives, weathering crises, adapting to changes in environment, ever re-creating itself.

Industrialism and the Traditional Family

When industrialism knocked on the door of Western civilization, it found a tightly feudal society composed of rigidly defined social classes bound to each other by a complicated set of rights and duties, the whole sanctified by a powerful Church. It also found mankind organized into a series of cohesive families, closely tied to the soil or to some location. This institution also was strongly supported by the Church. Within this feudal family, there was a patriarchal father who ruled his household in a thoroughly feudal manner; that is, he owed his family certain rights and exacted from them certain duties, including the duty to obey him. The wife in this family was subordinate to her husband, but in her own domain, whether farmstead or a house in the town, she was a person of prestige and of great influence over her children. The children were minor parts of the family. There were many of them in each family, except where disease carried them off, and no matter how great the affection of the parents for them en masse, they were relatively unimportant as individuals. Therefore childhood was not considered a time for play, but, rather, a time of preparation for life, a time for learning tasks and moving to new tasks when strength and agility would permit. Finally, to round out the complement of the family, there were the aged, who could no longer work but who were respected and perhaps a little feared.

This family was enmeshed in a large network of kinship ties. Close relationships were maintained with families related by marriage or by blood. Since families were stable and migration limited, all relatives were likely to be well known to each other. A whole neighborhood or even a village[1] might be made up of a few extended families. The extended family not only was the product of a stable society, it helped guarantee this stability. The extended family lent support to the smaller families within it; it enforced traditional standards and values.

Marriage in the traditional family was rarely a matter of choice. Marriages were arranged, and they were arranged not in terms of romantic attraction but in terms of socioeconomic realities. In a peasant village, the son of a peasant married the daughter of a peasant of equal status and wealth. The daughter of a nobleman was married to a nobleman whose rank would not disgrace her family. The traditional family, supported by the extended kin group, could be counted on to enforce, first, acceptance of the chosen mates, and then, to a certain degree, harmony within the home.

It is this type of family, or some version of it, which lies in the immediate background of most Americans. Either they are descended from peasant families of the traditional type; or they come from rural areas where a modified form of the traditional family is still

---

[1] This has been true even in the United States in the past. See James West, *Plainville, U.S.A.* (New York: Columbia University Press, 1945), pp. 57-69.

in existence. Even urban families of a few generations ago were not unlike the traditional family described above. Nor is this type of family extinct today. It continues to exist wherever industrialism has not penetrated, for instance, in India, or China, or sections of Latin America.

Industrialism quickly and permanently shattered this family form, and it continues to do so wherever it enters a region or a nation. It does so first, because it must break the ties of the family to land or location in order to fill cities with propertyless workers, dependent solely on the factories for their livings. Industrialism cannot even tolerate a deeply rooted urban family, for it requires a mobile population, mobile in both the social and geographical senses.

Secondly, industrialism is incompatible with traditional family relationships. It must use the labor of father, mother, adolescents, and even children on an equal plane; it has no affinity for the fine distinctions of status and authority in the traditional family. Industrialism separates the place of work from the place of family life, and in doing so it pulls parents away from children, husbands away from wives. It breaks up the continuity of the traditional family; in industrial society the family no longer can function as a face-to-face group except at comparatively rare times. Industrialism leads the individual to chafe at the bonds of the traditional family; children who can earn almost as much as their fathers, and who know as much, will not readily accept his authority. Nor will such children readily consent to marry those whom their parents have selected for them. Since the traditional family is not able to control marriages, its homogeneity and unity may be shattered with the introduction of spouses of differing nationalities, perhaps even of different religions.

Thirdly, industrialism has shattering effects on the extended family. The extended family is often scattered; the component parts of the extended family may live in different sections of the city, in different cities, sometimes even in different nations. Ties between relatives become looser—and, in many cases, disappear entirely. In turn, the weakening of the extended family still further weakens the smaller families.

Fourthly, industrialism radically changes the physical environment of the family and, as a result, induces certain changes in the family structure. The home is transferred from the country to the city or town, where living space is scarce. In the city homes often become crowded and unattractive and may positively repel family members. Outside the home are all the attractions of urban life; places of recreation, clubs, corner gangs, etc. The family tends to drift apart; the home becomes a place for meals and for sleeping, but other activities transpire outside the home.

Thus, in these and other ways, industrialism dissolves the hard lines of relationships in the traditional family. Does this mean that the family is doomed to disappear, as some have warned? From what we now know, nothing seems less likely. All the deep-lying psychological needs of men and women for family existence remain. What has changed is the *way* these needs can be filled in industrial society; what has changed is the form of the family—its structure and its inner relationships.

The General Form of the Industrial-Urban Family

There are two ways of looking at the form of the industrial-urban family. One may consider the general form of the industrial-urban family, that is, those elements which are common to *all* families of this type. Or one may consider the various subtypes of this general urban-industrial family. Here we shall do both; first we shall consider the general form of the family, and then we shall consider certain subtypes as *deviations* from this general form.

In general, various aspects of the industrial-urban family have been shaped by the needs of industrialism in various ways.[2] One striking peculiarity of the industrial-urban family is its isolation from other areas of society. As has been shown, the industrial-urban family is not embedded in a matrix of extended kin relationships. Relatively few urban families maintain close relationships with more than a handful of relatives not in the immediate family. This isolation of the family is reflected in our kinship terminology, which fails to distinguish between near or remote cousins, between paternal or maternal aunts, uncles, or grandparents.[3] For the industrial-urban family, most relatives outside the immediate family are alike.

---

[2] Other forces also have helped shape our family, for instance, the democratic ideology and the Judaeo-Christian tradition.

[3] Talcott Parsons, "The Social Structure of the Family," in Ruth Nanda

Another characteristic of urban-industrial families is that, to a degree unheard of in other cultures, the family is based on the conjugal relationship. Since the family no longer rests on ties to property, to location, to land, or to extended family, the stability of the family, its success or failure, depends on the compatibility of husband and wife. It is the ability of the husband and wife to adjust to each other, to compromise their difficulties, which is crucial in our family system. Since so much hinges on the conjugal relationship, mates must be chosen in terms of personal preference; e.g., in terms of romantic attraction, sexual compatibility, and personality affinity. Even if there were no reason of an ideological nature, it is doubtful whether a system of arranged marriages could work in our society.

Within this isolated, conjugal family, certain types of roles appear. Caution must be exercised here, because it is precisely in the area of roles and role playing that the greatest variations exist in our families. However, certain generalizations about these roles may be made.

In general, the modern family is marked by a relatively great degree of equality in its roles. For instance, the father is less of an authoritarian figure than in the patriarchal family; he cannot command the obedience of his wife or children to nearly the same degree that the patriarch could. The father of the industrial-urban family must adjust his personality to the emotional needs of his wife; he must, in a sense, cultivate the good will of his children. By the same token, the wife enjoys a relatively high status in our family system. Though her duties in the home remain largely traditional, these duties have been lightened by her relationship with her husband, by the easing of household drudgery through technological applications, and by the possibility of taking employment on the outside. Furthermore, to a greater degree than ever, the wife is close to and can influence her children.

The role of the child has been drastically altered. Still speaking generally, we may say that the child is less of an economic asset, and spread of contraceptive knowledge, has resulted in the reduction of

Anshen, ed., *The Family: Its Function and Destiny* (New York: Harper, 1949), p. 175.

number of children per family. The child thus has a better chance for survival and for health. At the same time, the child also has the opportunity to emerge as an individual in the family—if not an individual of equal status to the adults, at least one with definite rights. Childhood today involves not a dreary preparation for adult life but a separate culture of school and of recreation. Furthermore, the very fact of the relative scarcity of children in our families increases the emotional involvement of parents in their children; the child in our society is the object of a great deal of parental affection and concern.

Another important facet of the role structure of our families is the separation of place of work and the home. Unlike the peasant, who worked perhaps within sight of his home, the modern man goes to work; that is, he leaves his family for eight hours or more a day. Furthermore, what he does in his place of work is usually incomprehensible to his family or of little interest to them. Thus the child or the adolescent or the wife is cut off from the occupational world almost entirely. One consequence is that the father can no longer serve as a model for his son, or, at least, it is more difficult for him to do so; the result is that relatively few sons in our society consciously desire to emulate their fathers. Another consequence is that children are thrown upon their mother; it is she who must give them affection, care for them, and discipline them.

The functions of the family are also drastically altered under modern conditions. The family is no longer the main economic unit of society. Its productive functions have almost entirely disappeared. In the economic sphere, the family functions chiefly as a consuming unit and to motivate economic activity. Religious functions, recreational functions, even educational functions are appropriated by other institutions under modern conditions of urban life. On the other hand, the affectional function of the family gains new importance. In contrast to the impersonality, anonymity, and harshness of modern society, and not least in its industrial sector, are the warmth, tenderness, and intense personal qualities of family life. The fact that many marriages end in divorce because of the failure of the affectional function points up the importance of this function in the modern family.

Industry, then, affects the form of the modern family in many ways. The isolation of the family may be traced to the overriding demand of industry for mobility. The stress on the conjugal relationship is in turn related to the isolation of the family. The equality of roles is related to the employment opportunities opened by industry, as well as to the equalitarian ideology which is partly the result of industrialism. The functional nature of the family represents a compromise between the needs of industrialism and the emotional needs of humanity.

Industrially Influenced Families and Aspects of Family Living

The general features of the family described above are well-nigh universal in our society; they exist among families which are entirely outside the industrial sphere as well as among those which have direct connections with industry. The family form which we describe has become a part of our culture, which is itself in part a product of industrialism. But, in addition to this general influence on our family system, industry is directly influencing those families whose members are connected with industry.

In general the direct influence of industry on the family is bound up with the occupational structure of industry. This works in two ways. On the one hand, the particular occupation which an individual follows in industry determines many immediate aspects of family living. For instance, the occupation determines the amount of income which the family will live on, the amount of "living" which it can buy. Furthermore, occupation determines the amount of time which the job holder will spend in the home, whether that time will be in the night or in the day. Occupations create tensions and strains, as we have seen, which may be transferred to family life. Certain attitudes and values are created by occupational experience, and these may infiltrate family relationships in many subtle ways.

On the other hand, insofar as occupation determines class and status position, many indirect influences on family life are being felt. Class and status groups are, as we have seen, really subcultures in our society with indigenous habits, values, attitudes, speech, definitions of the situation, and so on. The fact that a given family belongs to a particular class or status group determines many structural and functional features of that family: the number of children in the family, the role of the father, the position of the mother, the role of the aged, the vulnerability of the family to crisis.

In the discussion that follows we shall concentrate on the influence of industry on . . . the formation of families and family structure. As we shall see, sometimes this influence is of the direct or "occupational" variety, sometimes it is indirect, mediated through class and status.

Families in the Labor Force: How many families are directly connected with industry by virtue of having one or more members working in industry? Unfortunately a precise estimate is not possible. It is known, however, that there are over 40 million families in the United States.[4] Over 31 million of these reside in urban areas; the rest, in rural nonfarm or rural farm areas. Of the total number of families, about 10 per cent have no member in the working force. About 56 per cent of the families have one person in the labor force, about 25½ per cent have two, 6½ per cent have three, and 2.2 per cent have four or more.[5] Thus a total of about 36 million families were connected with the labor force.

Using these figures, and from what we know of the composition of the working force, it may be estimated that about two-thirds of families have one or more members earning a wage or salary in a nonagricultural industry. In absolute figures, about 24 million families are connected with industry. Though the figures presented here are not precise, it can be clearly seen that a large proportion of American families have one or more members connected with industry.

The Formation of Families: We have seen that families in our society are formed through the "free choice" of men and women. This does not mean, however, that the formation of marriages in our society is purely a matter of chance physical attraction. On the contrary, it is strongly influenced by social and economic conditions. These conditions set limits within which "free choice" operates in the selection of marriage mates.

---

[4] U.S. Bureau of the Census, *Statistical Abstract of the United States: 1954,* p. 54, table 50.

[5] A. J. Jaffee and Charles D. Stewart, *Manpower Resources and Utilization* (New York: Wiley, 1951), p. 136, table 5.

Directly or indirectly, industry helps form the socioeconomic environment within which marriages are formed. In the first place, industry may have a *direct* effect on the formation of marriages, by the simple fact of bringing together large numbers of men and women where propinquity may exert its force. It can be shown with more concreteness that there is a high marriage rate between men and women in the same occupation or between men and women who come from the same occupational levels. Thus Sundal and McCormick in a study of marriage in Madison, Wisconsin, found that over 45 per cent of unskilled or semiskilled male workers married women who were operatives or domestic workers.[6] Centers found that 33 per cent of a national sample of business executives married women whose fathers were also businessmen; 26 per cent of the white-collar workers, 52 per cent of skilled workers, 48 per cent of the semiskilled, and 25 per cent of the unskilled likewise married women whose fathers were in the same occupational classes as themselves.[7] It is impossible to state to what extent these intra-occupational marriages are the result of direct contacts at work, and to what extent they reflect similar class and status backgrounds of the spouses. Probably both factors are at work here.

In the second place, industry affects the formation of marriages indirectly, through the medium of class and status. It has been shown that class and status are intimately linked to the occupational structure of industry. Therefore, if there is evidence of the influence of social stratification on marriage, there is, at the same time, evidence for the influence of industrialism on marriage. Such evidence exists. For instance, several studies have shown that a large number of marriages occur between men and women who live within a relatively short distance of each other. The pioneer study of Bossard showed that over 50 per cent of 5,000 applications for marriage made in Philadelphia in the early 1930's were between parties who

---

[6] A. Philip Sundal and Thomas C. McCormick, "Age at Marriage and Mate Selection: Madison, Wisconsin, 1937-1943," *American Sociological Review* 16:1 (1951), p. 43, table 5.

[7] Richard Centers, "Marital Selection and Occupational Strata," *The American Journal of Sociology* 54:6 (1949), p. 535, table 9.

lived within 20 blocks or less of each other; in fact, in over 12 per cent of the cases, the applicants gave the same address. Since people who live in the same neighborhood are likely to come from the same economic class and, though less certainly, from the same status group, there is evidence that these marriages took place between people with the same socioeconomic backgrounds.[8]

Further evidence of the prevalence of intraclass marriages may be found in the similarity of the financial situations of the parties to the marriage. Homogamy in financial background is, of course, implied in the similarity of occupational background, which has been described above. Scattered studies tend to support this deduction. For instance, a study of 1,000 engaged couples, largely middle-class, in Chicago showed a "moderate" degree of correlation between the financial standings of the parents of the couples.[9] Sundal and McCormick's study of Madison, Wisconsin, showed similarity in the assessed valuations of the homes from which married couples came.[10]

Finally, similarity in the amount and type of education of married couples supports the thesis of the similarity of the socioeconomic backgrounds of many spouses.[11] It was shown that education is a particularly sensitive index of socioeconomic position, because education is both the product of life chances and, at the same time, a major determinant of those chances.

From the evidence at hand, it may be concluded, therefore, that marriages in our society do not occur randomly. Marriages occur between people who are thrown together at work or who are brought together by their positions in the socal structure. In both ways,

---

[8] James H. S. Bossard, "Residential Propinquity as a Factor in Marriage Selection," *The American Journal of Sociology* 38:2 (1932), p. 221, table 2.

[9] Ernest W. Burgess and Paul Wallin, "Homogamy in Social Characteristics," *The American Journal of Sociology* 49:2 (1943), p. 113, table 1.

[10] Sundal and McCormick, p. 46, table 8.

[11] In a study of the married in New Haven, Conn., it was found that the men had in fact married women of equal or lower educational attainment. See August B. Hollingshead, *Elmtown's Youth* (New York: Wiley, 1949), pp. 625-627.

though to an undetermined degree, industrialism affects the formation of marriages in our society.

Status-Class Position and Family Structure

The influence of industrialism on families is not confined merely to their formation; in numerous direct and indirect ways industrialism helps to shape various *subtypes* of the American family. Subtypes of families occur in relation to regions, religions, ethnic groups, races, and other factors. The subtypes which are of interest to us deviate from the "ideal" American family in terms of their position in the class and status system, which in turn is, as we have seen, linked to industrialism.

Demographic Deviations: Certain demographic characteristics of American families vary in relation to position in the status-class system. This is true, for instance, of the *size* of families. Numerous studies have demonstrated an *inverse* relationship between status-class position, on the one hand, and fertility, on the other; that is, the "lower" classes have more children than the "upper" classes. . . .

Families are largest among "operatives and kindred workers"; families are smallest among professional and technical workers and among sales personnel. Similarly, an inverse relationship can be demonstrated between education and fertility, between rental paid for homes and fertility, and between fertility and other socioeconomic indices.[12] However, there is now some indication that the difference in size of families by socioeconomic status is beginning to decrease; indeed, for certain high-level occupations, the relationship has become a direct one, higher occupational levels tending to show larger families than somewhat lower occupational levels.

American families of differing socioeconomic status also show variations in the ages at which the spouses marry. However, here the relationship is a direct one; the higher the occupational position and the greater the money income, the later the age of mar-

---

12 Everett S. Lee and Anne S. Lee, "The Differential Fertility of the American Negro," *American Sociological Review* 17:4 (1952), p. 445, table 5; Clyde V. Kiser, "Fertility Trends and Differentials in the United States," *Journal of the American Statistical Association* 47:257 (1952), p. 43, fig. 5.

riage. Men of higher occupational levels tend to marry women nearer their own ages, while members of lower-ranking occupations tend to marry women further from their own age. Thus there is a median difference of 2.4 years in the ages of husbands and wives on the level of clerical workers, and a difference of 2.7 years in the ages of spouses on the "operative" level.[13] . . .

C. Commentary and Analysis

The industrial sociologist studies many other ways in which industry and the family are related. For example, in the remainder of his chapter "Industry and the Family," from which we have taken our selection, Schneider discusses industry and the role structure in family life, married women workers, children and old age. However, we have sufficient material to begin our theological (or Christian) reflection.

The simple yet profound fact which strikes us throughout Schneider's selection is that industry and the family are inextricably interrelated. The gradual changes in the world of industry have remolded the concept and the reality which we call "family." Schneider showed how industrialism shattered the form of the traditional family in its social and physical settings as well as in the relationships among the individual members of the family.

The radical human development of each individual's personality in its intellectual, social, cultural and emotional dimensions occurs within and through the family. We saw, for example, that the father no longer generally serves as the model for his son's life and career; in the family today mothers have a far greater effect on affective and disciplinary sides of the child's life; childhood today involves a "separate culture of school and recreation" outside the family.

It is clear from these few examples that when the structure of the family and the roles of the members of the family are modi-

---

[13] Paul C. Glick and Emmanuel Landau, "Age as a Factor in Marriage," *American Sociological Review* 15:4 (1950), p. 529, table 4.

fied then there necessarily follows a variation in the direction and path of human development. Such development is not necessarily deeper or shallower than before, neither is it necessarily more or less intense. The development is simply *different*. For example, the family today is more conscious than ever before of the value of education, so the child's and adult's attitudes toward school and college are different than a decade ago. Similarly, the relationships between father and children today are different from a generation ago. Again, the position of a nuclear family within the extended family is different, as is the role of the contemporary family within the contemporary community. The emphasis here is on *different*. The differences are fact, and it is upon facts that we must reflect.

The basic changes in the meaning of the family naturally result in modification of the theological and moral perspectives of the individual Christian. Hence the intimate relation between work and the family and human personality must not only be admitted but brought clearly into the foreground in examining Christian attitudes and patterns of behavior. True, the abstract meanings of justice and charity do not change; but the particular demands of justice and the concrete opportunities for kindness are different because of industry's modification of American family life. Likewise, the need for prayer and worship in the Christian life does not cease; but no one would claim that people today pray and worship as the peasants who built the cathedral at Chartres, or even as our Victorian forefathers did.

If the Christian is unable to modify the irrepressible movement of American industry, he can at least recognize the effect industry is having on the family and upon him through the family. These changes are continually coming about and require that the Christian, to live fully, must continually reevaluate the meaning of work in his own life and the influence which work and the world of industry is having upon him through the family.

Schneider pointed out that while religious, recreational and educational functions of the traditional family have been appropriated by other modern institutions, the affectional function of the family becomes of crucial importance.

In contrast to the impersonality, anonymity, and harshness

of modern society, and [this] not least in its industrial sector, are the warmth, tenderness, and intense personal qualities of family life. The fact that many marriages end in divorce because of the failure of the affectional function points up the importance of this function in the modern family.

The importance of the emotional life in the individual's psychological growth is the cornerstone of the structure of modern counseling centers and psychiatric clinics for individuals and families.

The impact of industry upon the family affects not only an individual's emotional maturity but also his social status, economic capabilities, personality development, educational growth, interpersonal attitudes. In short, most of the fundamental dimensions of the human person, hence of the Christian person, are molded and continually modified by the family as it is continually affected and reshaped by modern industry.

It is the task of each individual Christian to discover how his life is influenced by the world of work through the family's structure and function. Many of his attitudes toward life and work were essentially fashioned in the family in which he grew to manhood. His own work experience has helped to reinforce or modify these attitudes.

The outlook toward work and the family of a husband in his office is different from that of a housewife in her kitchen; the outlook of a third grader is different from that of a retired grandfather.

To take a concrete example, let us consider some of the facts and factors which the sociologist feels are important to the working husband in a middle-class family. First of all, the working husband in the middle class, because of his technologically complicated job, must usually try to construct a role within the family which has practically nothing to do with his work. And since the home centers essentially about the mother and her children, the man's role in this sphere becomes subordinate. Consequently, he often cannot be the role-model for his children, nor is his wife able strongly to identify with his work. Likewise, the rewards and problems of his occupational life are unsharable (Schneider, p. 437).

From this simple example of the working husband in the middle class, seen in the context of the entire Schneider selection, we have an indication of how industry and work have modified the formation and function of the American family and hence have encouraged and occasioned the redefinition of man's image of himself. At present the function of the family is, practically speaking, unclear; the importance of the family is unquestioned and hence there is much family research being done in the various branches of the social sciences.

One of the fundamental difficulties in establishing the function of the contemporary family is the situation where for the working individuals in the family, life has two centers — the workplace and the home. In a similar way, life for the school-goer has two foci, the school and the home. The working members and students in a family are sociologically conditioned to think and behave quite differently at work or school and at home. Life with a double center is a significant tendency in the growing secularization of the world.

For the family cannot be fully explained from within, simply on the biological grounds of procreation, mother instinct and the emotional feelings which exist between man and woman, parents and children. The family would not exist if there were no society in which it could come to be and develop. Conversely, the existence of families is a natural requirement for the existence of society. The relationship between society and the nuclear families which constitute it is not a static one, as we have seen; this relationship, as the interdependence of the family and work shows, is a dynamic process, a dialectic whose synthesis is never completely resolved but enters again and again into the dialectical process. This dialectic is possible, since society is somehow an independent entity and not merely a *collection* of families. Work shows us that man's meaning and vision of himself changes within the dialectic of family and society.

Questions for Discussion

1. What are the characteristics of the traditional family?
2. How did industrialism affect the traditional family? What has

happened to the form of the family, to inter-family relationships? To the extended family, to the family's physical environment?

3. What function of the family has emerged to take on new importance?

4. How does industrialism determine aspects of family living? Discuss both the direct and indirect influences of industry on marriage.

5. What example is given of the effect of work on a nuclear family? Does this fit specific situations in your experience? Discuss various situations you know.

III
WORK AND THE AGED

A. Prenote

After establishing in the last chapter the important mutual influences between industry and the family, this chapter and the next consider the two classes of family members who live on the periphery of the world of work, namely, the retired worker and the child. In discovering through the social sciences what meaning work holds for the elder citizen and for the child, we develop a deeper and broader insight into the full meaning of human effort as well as a more secure foundation upon which to base our theological reflection concerning the Christian in his world of work.

No members of the American community have been more strongly affected by the transformation of the family in contemporary society than the retired workers; none have tasted the bitterness of alienation more than the aged. During their working years their jobs had provided them with a rich source of friendship, experience and development on the social, psychological, cultural and economic levels of life. In the selection below, written especially for this book, Paula Zelipsky presents a survey of such meanings of work as seen from the eyes of the individual who is "beyond" work. She shows how our technological society forces the retired worker to face the problems of finding in leisure those psycho-social rewards which until now only work and the world of work could offer. When people retire, then alienation, feeling out of place and useless, are their commonest emotional reactions. From the findings of the social scientists, Miss Zelipsky shows the depths of the human rewards which work is able to offer an individual in the United States as well as the gaping hole which is often left in the life of a person who found his work a rewarding experience. It is not surprising that there are many who dread retirement and who look upon it as somehow the end of their lives. Hopefully, through a Christian vision of the meaning of life and work the findings of the human sciences can inspire us to give a new and fuller meaning to the work of the aged.

B. Selection: Aging and Retirement in Contemporary Society

Aging and its problems is a phenomenon and product of the industrial period. Not too many years ago the aged held positions of higher esteem and honor in society than they do today, for society was then family-centered. The essential economic activities were carried on by the extended family group. The older people were integral to the family, performing such tasks as entertaining and instructing the grandchildren, helping with the work around the house, watching a baby, or mending tools. Often the eldest members directed and dominated the whole familial group. With the exception of a few isolated agrarian cultures, the traditional kinship family with its provisions for the aged, usually as its leading force, has faded out of existence as a common phenomenon. Today there presides the nuclear family, father, mother and children, with little concern for the older people, who consequently withdraw or are excluded from the main stream of life, familial or otherwise, in industrial America. The source of this social change in the family lies in the combination of *industrialization,* demanding a population which is both geographically and socially mobile, and *individualism,* which encourages independence as a norm. Thus the nuclear family is expected to be independent of "ties" to relatives; this factor in turn isolates the aged from the family circle.

Industrialism and individualism, then, have fostered a new type of society, one which is mobile, independent, urban and youth-centered. Consequently, the very concept of old age is incongruous with the vigorously active technological society in which we live. Ironically, this society, with its improvements in the biological and medical sciences, has made a great community of older, retired Americans a reality. Retirement is a new way of life in more ways than one.

The formal entrance into old age is retirement, which comes at the end of a work career and is presented as a reward for a lifetime of labor. As such, retirement holds a powerful attraction for the workingman. On the other hand, retirement means a giving up of the economic, and especially extra-economic, rewards of involvement in the workaday world of industrial America. These approach-avoidance factors complicate adjustment to retirement.

We shall consider various definitions of aging and the present demographic distribution of the U.S. aged population. Afterward, we shall consider the meaning of retirement from work life in its social, economic, psychological and cultural dimensions.

Definitions of Old Age

To understand the problems that confront the aged of modern America it is necessary first to consider what is actually meant by old age in this society. There are at least four different definitions.

1. Biologically speaking, aging refers to the changes which take place in the cells, tissues, organs, or organism with the passage of time. Such changes include: an increase in the connective tissue of the organism, a gradual loss of elastic properties of connective tissue, a disappearance of cellular elements in the nervous system, reduction in the number of normally functioning cells, an increased proportion of fat, a decrease in oxygen utilization, a decrease in the amount of blood pumped by the heart under resting conditions, and so on.

2. In gerontology, on the other hand, the interest lies primarily with changes which occur in the individual between maturity and death, and with the factors which influence these changes. Such factors will include heredity, climatic differences and social customs, but especially the relationships between individuals and their reactions to one another and to their environment.

3. Industry and industrial society defines old age chronologically. This practice arises from the influence of pensions and retirement in the nation's economy. Retirement is designated at some specific

chronological age, usually sixty-five. This is in reality a poor measure of old age, despite its efficiency in our computerized world; for
no two individuals age biologically or socially at the same pace.
And while the chronological ages of two individuals may be identical, their ages anatomically, physiologically, psychologically and
socially may vary greatly. In a word, a chronological definition of
old age fails to take into account the fact that aging is a dynamic
phenomenon which affects each individual in a different way
physically and psychologically.

4. Behaviorally, aging may be defined as "the survival of a
growing number of people who have completed the traditional
adult roles of making a living and child-rearing." [1] This definition,
too, is inadequate, for it reveals only the role which the older person has completed, not the role in which he is now engaged. The
classification of the aged is negative; it is a non-role. This lack of
a positive definition of their role in society is one of the main problems the aged face today, for they find themselves enveloped in
a youth-centered society with no definite assigned position. Retirement is *un*-employment. So, although retirement is one of the
very few approved forms of unemployment which our society allows its male members, the lives of the retired are often lived
without direction, motivation, or goals.

Breakdown of Aged Population in the United States

One of the reasons why the problems of the aged have come
to the forefront is the increased number of older people. At the
turn of the century there were only three million Americans over
the age of sixty-five. Today, while the general population has
doubled, the number of those sixty-five and over has increased five
times.

According to Milton Barron in *The Aging American,* this increase is a result of a number of demographic factors. First, although the birth rate has been declining, this decrease has been
counterbalanced by a decline in the death rate. Second, millions

---

[1] Clark Tibbetts and Wilma Donahue, eds., *Aging in Today's Society* (Englewood Cliffs, N.J.: Prentice-Hall, 1960), p. 4.

of persons who previously would have died in infancy and childhood, especially from communicable diseases, now expect to live
about seventy years. Third, the lower birth rates up to 1940 increased the proportion of older people. Finally, the increase of
older people is a result of the vast immigration of young adults
to America which continued until the quota laws of the 1920's;
those immigrants who have survived are now numbered among
the chronologically aged. With the sharp drop in immigration because of the quota laws, there are no young immigrants offsetting
the growing proportion of older persons.

It is also of some importance to note that in general women live
longer than men. The reasons for the female longevity are only beginning to be explored. In the meantime, statistics assure us that
American women on the average live more than six years longer
than American men.

In looking at the aging population as a whole we see: (1) that
the nation is growing older, so that for every 100 persons aged
65-69 in 1980 it is estimated there will be 150 persons aged 70
and over; (2) that the population is and will remain predominantly
white, with the predominance ever more marked among the aged;
(3) that the majority of the population will be women, with the
proportion even more heavily in favor of the women among persons aged 70 and over; (4) that the aged are frequently no longer
part of a family group, since most of the women and one-third of
the men are widowed, divorced or single.

The places of residence of the aged are not evenly distributed
throughout the United States. The proportion of them is greatest in
the Midwestern and the New England states. The Northeastern
as well as the Pacific coast states have a high proportion of old
people, as does Florida. The Western and Southern states have a
relatively low proportion of older people.

The geographic variance results in part from the birth and death
rates of the respective areas. A high birth rate indicates a higher
proportion of children which offsets the proportion of older resi-
dents. To some extent interstate migration has influenced this
proportion, for older people seldom leave their home state. It is
rather the young adults who migrate, leaving behind their parents;
for mobility is more characteristic of youth than of old age.

When older people do migrate they not only move southward and westward but also from the suburbs and rural areas to villages and cities. The reasons for this migration according to Barron, are usually the following: (1) the physiological benefit of the warmer climate, (2) lack or loss of ownership and control of property, (3) lack of a definite place for the aged in the community's social structure, stemming from prejudice against old age, especially in youth-centered suburbs, (4) the establishment of social security assuring a modest source of income independent of place of residence, (5) breakdown of two- or three-generation family units for those elderly couples who wish to migrate.

Retirement: Social Aspect

Retirement is a significant change for it permeates one's entire life in practically all its dimensions. On the social side, many gerontologists support the idea that retirement leads to maladjustment. They contend that our industrial society has cultural standards and values which emphasize the importance of work; hence, no role is an adequate or satisfactory substitute for the role of worker.

In *Civilization and Its Discontents* Freud defines work as a way of life, the bond with reality, the means of communal contact which serves to identify the individual with society and which functions as a high form of sublimation, helping to make man a social, civilized being.

The reaction to a loss of a job depends on many different factors and much is based on the individual's previous development. This reaction also depends on whether or not the individual was prepared for retirement and if he had anticipated it. If he had anticipated it, he probably also had some substitute in mind such as another job, a hobby, travel or study. Reaction and adjustment to retirement depends on the functional capacity the individual still retains.

A differentiation should be made at this point between the middle class and the "working" class. Sociological studies show that middle-class people value and practice foresight and conformity more than the working class. Thus, we can expect on the part of the middle-class aged a better preparation and a stronger motive for adjustment to retirement. But evidence indicates that the social and cultural values of work and the man who works are so strong that the aged in America are more inclined to identify themselves with the "working" class than any other social stratum; hence, there is a general neglect of preparing for retirement and a lack of interest in counseling programs for retirement. In observing a counseling program for foreign-born and semiskilled manual workers, Barron found that they reacted negatively to any discussion of hobbies and considered this word to be synonymous with childish play. Whatever preparation and adjustment there is seems to be associated with middle-class psychology rather than the mentality of the industrial worker.[2]

At the University of Chicago, Burgess also concluded, in a study of the occupational differences in attitudes toward aging and retirement, that there is a great difference between retirement planning of the upper occupational group and that of the manual worker. The supervisory-professional people have a more favorable attitude toward aging and retirement while the manual worker tends to avoid facing financial planning, retirement preparation, social adjustment and job satisfaction. The conclusion drawn from this study was that the two groups should have different retirement programs. The upper level group needs an opportunity to reinterpret their knowledge, while another program is needed to help the manual worker discover that retirement can be genuinely meaningful.[3]

Therefore, social maladjustment cannot be attributed to retirement in every case, for there are too many variables and individual differences to contend with. One must always remember the value-position which work holds in this society and the effect produced by the loss of that job.

Retirement: Psychological Aspect

When an individual passes from the working life to retirement,

---

[2] Milton L. Barron, *The Aging American* (New York: Crowell, 1961), pp. 72-3.
[3] Kurt Wolff, *The Biological, Sociological and Psychological Aspects of Aging* (Springfield, Ill.: Charles C. Thomas, 1959), p. 29.

he passes into a new way of life. The elderly man who has filled his day with eight hours of work for many years must now find new ways of living these eight hours daily. For most people, but especially for those with lower socioeconomic status, the primary meaning of work is earning a living. But for just about all classes of individuals work has more than an economic aspect. For example, work gives a person a chance to be useful, to be of service to others; work develops self-respect, prestige and gains for the worker the respect of others; work provides a setting for forming a group of friends and associates; work provides something to do for eight hours a day and forms a reference point of one's life; finally, work often gives life a purpose and direction, providing openings for advancement and goals to be achieved.

As we ascend the ladder of occupations and skills these extra-financial meanings of work assume greater importance. To varying degrees for all types of workers, the job is a source of interesting and purposeful activity and a source of intrinsic enjoyment. Among the groups of workers studied by Friedman and Havighurst, the individual workers who stressed the value of extra-economic meanings of work were also the ones least likely to want to retire at age sixty-five.[4]

In the same study the authors found also that a large majority of men who worked primarily to earn a living looked forward to retiring at sixty-five. It was among such workers that the negative psychological values of work were prominent, e.g., uncreative and self-demeaning daily routine, exhausting and dangerous tasks, distasteful and uninteresting labor and little opportunity for the service of others.

In any case, the retired worker faces a problem of psychological adjustment. Adjustment may be defined, according to Robert Havighurst, as a complex harmony of needs, interests and emotions changing to meet the changing situation as a person moves through life. In addition to the adjustment demanded by the cessation of

---

[4] Eugene A. Friedman and Robert J. Havighurst, et al., *The Meaning of Work and Retirement* (Chicago: University of Chicago, 1954), pp. 182-3.

the daily occupation, old age brings with it many situations for which a change in needs, interests and emotions is necessary.

The wife must learn new living patterns with her husband at home much more of the time. It is necessary to readjust certain emotional relationships with one's friends and associates. Often for the older person there is a loss in the number of social contacts. The aged person's own increasing rigidity and insistence on regularity often limits social contacts. Physical difficulties, too, may make the maintenance of friendship difficult. If one must change his home, he must look forward to meeting and entertaining new friends, which is a difficulty for older individuals. Finally, the retired individual may become resentful of the younger generation by whom one feels himself displaced in the social world.

The loss of a spouse, especially for a woman, is likely to result in a marked psychological reaction, for this event often results in a loss of home, a serious economic change and an implication of one's own nearness to death. Above all, it is necessary after the death of one's spouse to readjust certain emotional relationships and to rechannel one's feelings of tenderness and affection to others and find someone to supply one's own need for love.

A new relationship between parents and adult children must be found. No longer should this be a relationship of authority on the part of the parent but rather a relationship characteristic of two adult persons. Difficulties arise when the retired parent fails to realize the change in the situation or refuses to recognize the change.

Economic stability and good health are favorable factors to good adjustment in old age. Similarly, findings of a study of institutionalized aged people indicated that religious faith and experience are related to good personal adjustment, but they do not necessarily indicate that this is a causal relationship. A large number of variables operate in affecting adjustment to old age. Religion is only one of these variables, but present knowledge seems to indicate that it is an important factor.[5]

---

[5] David O. Moberg, "Christian Religion and Personal Adjustment in Old Age," *American Sociological Review* 18 (February, 1953), p. 90.

Retirement: Cultural Aspect

It is clear that at the present time, certain cultural values in the social environment of the United States adversely affect older people. We are at present in a period of culture-value transition. One of the principal problems of retirement and old age is for the individual to secure those extra-economic values that work offers, and secure them through leisure-time activity. Some of these factors are: (1) social participation, friendships, membership in formal and informal associations; (2) interesting experiences and the opportunity for creative self-expression; (3) routinization of life-activity, i.e., something to do that helps the time pass; (4) sources of self-respect. The older person must learn to satisfy these work-created needs through leisure-time activity.

The problem is a cultural one, for the definition our society has given to "play" or leisure is "a rest from the burden of work." In our affluent world of abundance there is slowly emerging the cultural principle of the *equivalence of work and play,* where the values of play can be achieved through work and those of work through play. This principle of "equivalence" is not yet a part of the cultural system in our work-centered society, but when it is "discovered" by the nation as a whole, some of the problems of retirement and old age will be solved, provided economic security is also generally achieved.[6]

Retirement: Economic Aspect

Retirement is often a concern to people growing old because of economic difficulties that result from the loss of full-employment income. Ideally, personal savings should supplement the drop in income brought about by retirement, but, in reality, most elderly people have insufficient savings. The income provided by social security and pension checks rarely exceeds fifty percent of the pre-retirement income; more often this income is in the range of thirty or forty percent of the previous earnings. Yet most working-class people at middle age would rather enjoy consumer goods today than build a savings fund for retirement in the future. Sav-

---

[6] Friedman and Havighurst, p. 192.

ings may be sufficient for emergencies but are seldom adequate for the years of day to day living which may be expected during retirement. Furthermore, inflation has devalued the savings which working people had expected would be sufficient to carry them through the later years.

A nationwide sample survey of old-age and survivors' insurance beneficiaries showed that in 1951 about sixty percent of the old-age beneficiaries had some savings other than real estate. However, only thirteen percent had at least $5,000. Home ownership for most families with assets was the major significant asset. Of the married men about two-thirds owned their own homes, eighty percent free of mortgage. Those who owned their homes generally were the ones who had some additional savings. About two-thirds of the old-age beneficiaries, however, had no assets other than real estate or had some assets amounting to less than $1,000. One-fourth of these had no assets whatsoever.

Some insurance companies advertise annuities which are supposed to assure economic security in later life, but a modest annuity of $75 per month beginning with age sixty-five requires a man to have an accumulation of $11,900, and since women live longer, a woman would require an accumulation of about $13,900. With the average worker's income this savings is never, or seldom, amassed, for his savings are usually drained during illness, unemployment, and in bringing up his children.[7]

The sources of income for the aged are not a few. In June, 1956, 45 percent of the aged were receiving social security benefits as income, while 29 percent secured their income from their employment. Public old-age assistance gave another 16 percent their income while about 12 percent of these older people were receiving benefits from programs for veterans or for retired railroad and government workers. About 5 or 6 percent were receiving private insurance or annuity payments and 6 percent were under private retirement plans. An unknown percentage were receiving income from investments and contributions from children and

---

[7] Robert M. Ball, "The Economic Situation of the Aged," *Health in the Later Years,* John M. Maclachlan, ed. (Gainesville: University of Florida, 1953), pp. 49-50.

other relatives. Some, primarily widows, had no cash income at all and were being supported by children or other relatives.[8]

There has been much discussion on the ability of adult children to care for their aging parents in today's society. Some facts to keep in mind are the following: (1) The total burden of support of aged parents by children is on the continuing increase due to the larger numbers of aged in the population and the increased life-expectancy. (2) The number of adult children of the aged per family has declined, leaving a smaller number to assume support for aged parents. (3) Under urban conditions, fewer adult married children have an extra room to house an aged parent and find it financially impossible to move to larger quarters. (4) Children of the aged today have more children of their own together with increasing costs for rearing and education. In general, the economic costs to support parents in urban conditions is high.[9]

The economic situation points up the incongruity of the situation where the life expectancy is lengthened while working life is shortened. There has been a transition from the self-employment pattern of rural society to the industrial urban economy. During this transition the value of the individual older worker has declined. Now the worker is given a longer life without sufficient means to sustain it.

Closely associated with the economic problems of the aged are their problems of health and medical care. With age there is usually a failing of health and also a decreasing income from which medical aid must be financed. Actually, the number of days annually of inactivity because of acute illness, injury or chronic disability is two-and-one-half times as large for those 65 and over (43 days) as for those younger (17 days). The number of days of confinement to bed is double for older persons, 14 days for those over 65 and 7 for others. Also, the older person con-

---

[8] Barron, p. 42.

[9] Ernest W. Burgess, "The Older Generation and the Family," *The New Frontiers of Aging,* Wilma Donahue and Clark Tibbetts, eds. (Ann Arbor: University of Michigan, 1957), pp. 165-6.

sults a physician about 6.8 times a year, on the average, compared to a rate of 4.8 consultations for a person under 65.[10]

Not only are health services required more by aged persons, but the problem of paying for them is an acute one for an older person. In a study sponsored by the Health Information Foundation and conducted by the National Opinion Research Center of the University of Chicago, it was shown that the per-person costs of all kinds of medical services increase with age. For example, for the age group 0-5 years and 65 and over, respectively, the annual charges per person were $5 and $25 for hospital services, $15 and $36 for physician's services, and $6 and $22 for medicines. Also in another study of couples 65 and over who were receiving old-age and survivors' benefits, it was shown that one-fourth of these people had medical and hospital bills of more than $200 per year.[11]

Conclusion

It is clear that the problem of old age in a youth-centered industrial society is a complex and difficult one. The financial problems are crucial. These are receiving attention from the federal government and other agencies. Fulfillment of the extra-financial meanings of an active work life, i.e., those on the social, cultural and psychological levels, are much harder to satisfy. For our nation as a whole has not learned to retire. Many workers who looked forward to retirement as well as those who did not want to retire at 65 were unable to adjust to this new way of life. Perhaps, in the long run, the principle of equivalence of work and play will enter our cultural patterns and provide an adequate vehicle for the transition into the life of the retired.

At present, the most favorable factors to adjustment according to a study by Shanas are:

---

[10] Lenore A. Epstein and James C. Callison, "Financing Health Care for the Aged," *Law and Contemporary Problems* 27 (Winter 1962), p. 118.

[11] Marion T. Loftin, "The Health of the Aged Population," in Irving L. Webber, ed., *Aging: A Current Appraisal* (Gainesville: University of Florida, 1956), p. 130-1.

. . . being native white, happily married and living with the spouse, living in a place of one's choice and maintaining good family relationships. It is important to have friends, at least twenty-five of them, with more than ten intimate friends. Health should be good, at least fair, with less than four physical problems. Six or more leisure-time activities, at least one hobby, and some daily reading added to this. It helps to belong to at least one organization and attend at least once a month. In addition, the well-adjusted people attend church at least once a week, read the Bible regularly, and listen to radio church services. Lack of decline in health, number of friends, and amount of social participation are favorable signs. They must also have enough money to get along and have a feeling of permanent economic security.[12]

C. Commentary and Analysis

It is already clear from the first two selections in this anthology that there are many other variables besides productivity and pay which make their impact upon the individual in his world of work. Work and a work-life imply and supply a whole network of underlying values and motivations, as Zelipsky's article pointed out in her psycho-social survey of the meaning of work in the eyes of those who are retired.

It is the Christian's task to understand and evaluate these subsurface meanings and rewards and to place them into a picture of Christian interaction with the created world.

Although the study of work and retirement brings into focus the meanings and rewards of work in general, it is particularly necessary, in the light of the ever-growing sub-culture (or supra-culture) of elderly people, that the Chrstian reflect upon the place of the older persons in his life. First of all, every individual is aware that there are or soon will be older people involved in his life, either

---

[12] E. Shanas, "The Personal Adjustment of Recipients of Old Age Assistance," *Journal of Gerontology* 5 (1950), pp. 249-53.

as members of his family or household, perhaps as neighbors or only acquaintances. Certainly in the area of occupational employment and daily work the attitudes of the aged will differ from those of the young. The desire on the part of the retired individual to be useful, to have a purpose, to establish new social relationships, to maintain a certain degree of independence and privacy must be understood and acknowledged. Also it must be understood that such qualities previously were functions of the work-life. Providing avenues to these rewards for an older person demands much creative thinking, to make activities inviting, satisfying and productive. Clearly, the principle of the equivalence of work and play becomes important here.

Secondly, there are implications and obligations which the findings in this study of the aging place upon the worker who is approaching retirement. It would seem that the earlier one understands the values and rewards which his occupation brings to him, the more likely such a worker will be able to meet retirement properly, that is, not with a spirit of defeatist resignation but with a creative and curious eagerness, which should be the hallmark of the Christian who relishes the gift of life.

Thirdly, the retired worker himself can try to understand and re-evaluate his way of life as senior citizen of the contemporary world. Today retirement is a way of life; this is a new historical phenomenon. To understand himself the elderly person should ask himself why he behaves the way he does, why he reacts bright-eyed to some things and sour-faced to others, why he is resentful toward certain people and impatient in certain situations. In learning his likes and dislikes, he rediscovers himself. He should learn why he now "ticks" the way he does and how the younger people around him think and behave. Christian love is helpless unless it is based on knowledge; one's love for another will grow in proportion to the growth in one's understanding of the other.

Looked at from another angle, the growing number of older people offers possibilities for the development of the world, which were never before dreamed of. Such a statement may seem to be a rather surprising claim in our youth-centered world. But perhaps the principle of the equivalence of work and play has far deeper meanings for the growth of human sensitivity and understanding than simply as a principle for filling a gap in a retired person's life with aimless activity and games to pass the time away.

Perhaps we are hiding away in nursing homes and back rooms an army of experienced men and women who could hold a valuable place on the frontiers of creativity in the arts and sciences and in the very basic skill of full human and Christian living. Why can't we look upon our older people as a national resource of intelligent experience and potential, which is for the most part lying untapped, forgotten, needing only the proper incentive and invitation to come to light? No one who has made the smallest effort to obtain the friendship or cooperation of an older person can deny the eagerness with which the older person often responds.

Here lies a tremendous challenge, a preeminently Christian challenge, in the world of work. It demands on the part of the younger Christian a re-evaluation of many cultural prejudices concerning older people in a nation where youth and youthfulness reign. It demands a clear understanding of the motivations and rewards that accrue to the worker through his life and activity and that are often lacking in the life of retirement. It demands the communication of this psycho-social insight by the younger person to the retired worker himself, which communication establishes a necessary bond of understanding between the two age groups and upon which is built a bridge of trust, communication and cooperation. It demands a degree of concern from both sides which embraces the fresh insights of the young person and the well-earned experience of the retired worker. It demands a smiling patience on the part of the young worker and a hard-to-come-by openness to new ideas on the part of the older individual.

History books tell of men and women, like Benjamin Franklin and Winston Churchill, who have changed the course of the world after "retirement," individuals who refused to become museum pieces at sixty-five. These are exceptional personalities whose dynamism scorned the back-porch rocking chair, who made of old age a period of fullest blossoming, despite the cultural and social demands that they retire gracefully. There are today, however, millions of older people who need the invitation of the younger members of society to continue to work and contribute, who need the encouragement of others to form communities of older people who continue to look forward and find ways of being productive members of society.

Miss Zelipsky's article simply brings into sharper focus the fact that no human being wants to feel useless and left out. The Christian attitude toward man in the world assures us that no one is useless and that all men are to be embraced with love and understanding in the Christian community. To translate this Christian assurance into reality in the world of work, especially for the retired, is the challenge which faces both young and old together. Christians must point out to the modern world that it has made a serious mistake in burying the "talent" of the aging community, that community which—ironically—modern medical science itself has given us. Christians must point out this mistake not in the taunting supercilious way we sometimes do, which does nothing but irritate, but in a positive and concrete way, by using our minds and energies actually to rediscover and re-employ the older members of our society, to share insights with them, to work together with them, to profit from the treasures they have accumulated and which lie hidden in their hearts and minds.

Another important observation for reflection is the growing emphasis upon leisure and the crucial importance of leisure activities. The principle of the equivalence of work and play for the retired worker is clearly essential in this context. Furthermore, with the work-week growing shorter and shorter, almost all adults will be faced with the problem of how to use more leisure time and each adult in this situation, like the retired worker, will have to learn to obtain his work-rewards from his leisure activities. Another obvious implication of the trend toward leisure is in the education of children. Children will have to learn from the very beginning how to reap human values and meanings not only from their work but also from their play, not only while they are children but especially when they become adults.

Much Christian reflection is needed upon this principle of equivalence. It is capable of development, since the variables in its equation are functions of culture and society. The facts of work in today's world and in the life of the contemporary Christian demand the development of this principle. In our discussion we have tried to point out ways of approach for such development.

Questions for Discussion

1. Why is a study of the retired worker important? What two influences are responsible for the isolation of the aged from the family circle?
2. What four definitions of old age are offered by Miss Zelipsky? Why have the problems of the aged become so apparent? What factors are important to note in the increase in the aged population?
3. What are some of the social and psychological effects of retirement on the individual? What differences can be distinguished between the middle class and the working class in adjustment to retirement?
4. What is meant by the principle of equivalence of work and play? What significance does this principle have for the aged? What are some of the economic aspects of retirement for the aged?
5. In the light of this study, what are some of the implications and possibilities for the present and future place of the aged in society?

IV
WORK AND THE CHILD

A. Prenote

We do not usually associate work and children. The child, we feel, is luckily free from the need to work. We know that soon enough he will have to go out and earn a living. Now, however, he is fortunate to be a carefree individual, totally dependent upon his family for all his needs.

If we maintain the opinion that the aim of all work is to produce something "practical" (and this is the ordinary adult's concept of work), then the child and his "work" finds no place alongside the lawyer, the farmer or the mechanic. For the child's work is "to create the adult," to become. Maria Montessori, first woman medical student and M.D. in Italy, recognized early in this century the simple fact that the goal of the incessant daily activity of the child is precisely "to create the man."

Important as the child's work is, Montessori feels, this importance has never yet been fully recognized by society, probably because the child produces nothing visible to society—except himself.

All educationists recognize that intellects and intellectual techniques must be developed in the child. But, in addition, the various sensory-motor capacities of the human body as well as the social techniques of interpersonal relationships should receive increasing attention from the students of child education. There is much need for a deeper understanding of communication on all levels of existence, intellectual as well as emotional. Adolescents, especially, need further development and training in the verbal and non-verbal languages of interpersonal sharing. With proper childhood training, the tremendous powers of the senses of sight, sound and touch can be opened into whole worlds of intellectual and aesthetic appreciation. Montessori and Jean Piaget have been pioneers in this regard.

In the selection for this chapter Dr. E. Mortimer Standing, who worked for thirty years in close collaboration with Montessori, presents some of the insights of Montessori concerning the work of the child and its importance, comparing it to the work of the adult. The passage is taken from Standing's *Maria Montessori, Her Life and Work* (New York: Mentor Omega, 1962), pp. 141-154.

B. Selection: The "Work" of the Child—
The Creation of the Adult

A Comparison

Let us suppose we are down by the seashore, and we come across a workman filling a cart with sand; and near him is a small boy similarly engaged filling his toy wheelbarrow. Outwardly, both the child and adult are doing the same work. Now suppose I go up to the man and make the suggestion that I should do this work for him, and offer to take over his spade; he will probably think I am a bit eccentric. But if he comes to realize that I am really in earnest (and not a dangerous lunatic) he would probably say, "Okay, mister, if you really want to." He would then sit down and smoke a pipe in peace, meditating the while that there is no accounting for tastes. Now if I similarly approached the small boy, and—offering to take his spade—said, "Let me do that for you," do you think he would let me? The chances are a hundred to one that he would flatly refuse; and if I persisted the young fellow would probably defend himself from my help with great determination.

Furthermore, if we were to watch the small boy continuing at his work we should quite likely see that—when he had filled his wheelbarrow—he would just empty it and begin the process of refilling it all over again; and so on indefinitely. On the other hand, if, having finished filling the man's cart, I were to empty all the sand out again so that he had to begin the job over again from the start, I should probably find our relations would become considerably strained!

External and Internal Aim

Here we discern a great difference between the work of the adult and the work of the child, which we can express thus: the adult works with an external aim, to accomplish some change in his environment—in this case to fill the cart with sand for building purposes. But it is not so with the child's work. If his real aim was to fill his barrow with sand, why does he empty it again as soon as it is filled—to begin the "work" all over again?

Take another example. A lady was watching a small child slowly and laboriously buttoning up a very long pair of gaiters. She longed to help; but remembering Dr. Montessori's admonition to let children help themselves she resisted the impulse. Higher and higher up the legs toiled the little fingers till at last the top buttons were reached, and the lady heaved a sigh of relief. Imagine her astonishment when the child immediately began to undo all the buttons, and started the whole business *da capo*.

The same sort of thing happens every day in a Montessori school. You may see a child of three-and-a-half take all the ten cylinders out of their sockets and replace them a dozen times; and very likely she will do the same thing tomorrow; and perhaps every day for a week. If the aim of her work was to replace the cylinders, doing it once would have sufficed. In a school in Holland I once saw a little queue of children all waiting to polish the *same* brasses! "We adults don't fritter our energies away like that! We work to finish. The best runner is the one who gets there first; the best seamstress who sews most quickly; the best charwoman who gets through her work most speedily. 'She is a quick worker,' we say with praise."

Not so the child. He seems in no hurry to finish his work, and will repeat it, quite uselessly it seems to us. But it only seems useless to us because we are judging the child's work by our adult standards. The aim of the child's work is not external but internal. He works in order to grow. You cannot therefore see visibly the end for which he is expending all these labors. It is something remote, hidden in the obscurity of the future. Indefatigably, irresistibly, unceasingly, joyfully, the child is working to create the adult, the man-that-is-to-be.

The distant end for which the child is working is not of course consciously present to him; but the serene joy which we see in his expression indicates the satisfaction of a profound need of life. The child who is happy filling his bucket, washing a table, working with the cylinders, arranging the color tablets, counting, the number of rods—or whatever it may be—is obeying certain laws of growth— "inner directives": hence his contentment. As Montessori says, "Blessed is the child who has the joy of obeying in a manner exact, though unconscious, those divine forces which are in him. His is the joy of the creator. If from the newborn baby, helpless and unconscious, dumb, unable to raise itself, comes forth the individual adult with perfected form, with a mind enriched with all the acquisitions of his psychic life, radiant with the light of the spirit, this is the child's doing. For it is the child who builds the man."

Work and Environment

The work both of the child and of the adult has a definite relationship to the environment. We may say that the adult works to perfect his environment, whereas the child works to perfect himself, using the environment as the means. The adult—just because he is an adult—is no longer developing; he has reached the norm of the species; but the child is a being in a constant state of transformation. He is progressing, step by step, toward a more advanced state of being; and each new stage of development is marked by a new phase of this inwardly creative commerce with the environment, which we call work.

The Different Rhythm of the Child's Work

The more carefully we study the nature of the child's work the more clearly do we realize how profoundly it differs from that of the adult. So much so indeed that it is only the limitation of language that obliges us to use the same word. On more than one occasion I have heard Montessori complaining that, in order accurately to describe the child's nature and his activities, we need a "new vocabulary," since the accepted meanings of the words we are forced to use are often more of a hindrance than a help. And here we have a case in point.

For this reason we must analyze the matter a little further. As a corollary to the contrast already noted (between the nature of the work of the child and that of the adult) there arises another difference—in the inner rhythm or mental tempo which accompanies the two forms of work. A few examples will make the point clear. It is not uncommon to observe that a child of three-and-a-half who wants to work with the ten cubes of the pink tower on a rug on the floor will make ten separate journeys from the cupboard to the rug—one complete journey all across the room, in and out among the little tables, for each separate cube, even for the smallest. He could quite easily have taken two or three cubes together to save time and effort. An adult, or even a boy of seven years, would never act in that way. Or again, if you observe children carrying out the exercises of practical life you will see the same sort of thing. How slow they are, how unreasonable in their expenditure of effort! Take for instance the business of washing their hands. What an unconscionable time they take over it! How they seem to dwell, with a sort of inner relish, over each separate action, each little step in the process! Very slowly and deliberately, they will begin by turning up their sleeves, as if the whole morning was before them. How slowly—how caressingly—they will wash each separate finger—often pausing to look at their hands as though in contemplation—giving to each of the thirty different stages in this action as much interest and attention as a Benedictine monk performing a complicated liturgical ceremony.

To us adults it is a torment simply to watch this imperturbable leisureliness. We can hardly refrain from rushing in and taking over the action ourselves in order to get it finished and done with.

Why do we feel like this? Simply because the whole work-rhythm and tempo of our lives is different from theirs. All the time we cannot help envisaging in our mind's eye the completed action towards which we are moving. Inevitably we hasten towards this end as quickly and as economically as possible. The future of our day, week, year, lies all mapped out before us with their allotted tasks; while we, impelled by an inner tension, press onward to their fulfillment, our "present" forever leaning over into an urgent "future."

But it is not so with the child. He lives in a sort of everlasting present. He does not hurry as we do towards the end of the action, because for him the end of the action *is the action itself.* His whole being is expressed in his work; he loves it, lives it, rejoices in it, perseveres in it, repeats it—*because it is the means by which he is perfecting himself.*

It requires a real effort of imagination on our part to free ourselves from our own rhythm of work and project ourselves into his. We are always saying to these poor creatures: "Hurry up!" "Dear me, how slow you are!" or (worse still) "Here, let me do that for you!" Yet our efforts are as futile as those of the man on whose tombstone was carved "Here lies the man who tried to hustle the East." It is equally futile to try to hustle the work of the child. "He cannot be twenty before he is twenty." Nature has fixed his program; and you cannot change it; for, as Montessori says, "He is following the timetable like the most diligent scholar in the world—following it with the unshakable constancy of the stars in their courses."

Respecting the Child's Rhythm of Life

One of the first essentials for any adult who wishes to help small children is to learn to respect the different rhythm of their lives, instead of trying to speed it up, in the vain hope of making it synchronize with ours. To illustrate this point Montessori relates the following anecdote. One day she was watching a child of about five years composing the numbers 1—100 with the number frame. This is a material not unlike those wooden frames one sees put up in churches to indicate the numbers of the hymns to be sung. The child was patiently putting the cards in and taking them out. She had before her the task of separately composing each number from 1—100. To Montessori it seemed a dreadfully slow and long-drawn-out business. So, thinking she could help the child to arrive more quickly at its goal—which she took to be the number 100—she began asking her to compose some numbers further on, skipping out others to accelerate the process. The child submitted to her suggestions for some time with quiet patience, obediently doing what she was asked to do. Then, as if she could stand it no longer, she said, politely but firmly, "Please will you go away and let me do it my own way." Whereupon the little girl went back to the point in the number series where she had been interrupted; and carried on from there at the same tempo as before. "I felt justly rebuked," said Montessori, "for my stupidity. I had made the mistake of thinking the child's interest lay in getting to the end of the process and not in the process itself." This reminds one of R. L. Stevenson's remark: "To travel hopefully is a better thing than to arrive."

The Child, the Mystic, and the Artist

The inner rhythm of the child's life in some ways resembles that of a mystic; for both may be said to live in a sort of "eternal now." The contemplation of the mystic does not produce anything practical outside himself—it is an end in itself—and the end is self-perfection. Having become "as a little child," he is liberated from the hustle and bustle of adult life (this *vorticoso diventare*) with its ever-quickening tempo. The reason why the great liturgical ceremonies of the Church seem to us at times so long-drawn-out and tedious is just the same—i.e., because we are still clinging to the hurrying tempo of our everyday living. We have not been able to lift ourselves into the majestic rhythm of those actions which savor more of eternity than of time.

The child resembles the artist, too, as well as the mystic; because he has the task of creating a great masterpiece—which is the man-to-be. That is why you can no more hurry him than you can hurry on the work of an artist. If you think an artist can be hurried, read the story of the impatient Father Prior who tried to hustle Leonardo da Vinci into finishing the painting of his famous Last Supper.

Distorted Modern Ideas of Work

In the book of Genesis we read how God created the world from the formless void; and man from the dust of the earth. Something similar happens in the development of every individual. As Margaret Drummond used to say, "In every child the world begins anew."

Our modern industrialized society, according to Montessori, has lost all true sense of the value and meaning of work. This is partly because, in the present state of society, division of labor as we know it rests on false foundations; it is the result of the unchecked possessiveness of whole groups of men. Love of possession and love of power are "deviations" from the normal. It is these which have brought about a social condition in which some do no work at all, or very little, but live parasitically on the labors of others. "Work," says Montessori, "is so truly the natural expression of 'normalized' mankind (each species living on earth has its 'cosmic mission') that man's true name should be *homo laborans* rather than *homo sapiens!* But, alas, as things are at present, most persons have lost this 'instinct of the species.' It is only in persons of exceptional power—the geniuses—that this love of work persists as an irresistible impulse, surviving in spite of the unhappy conditions which have smothered it in the majority. Such are for example the artists, discoverers, explorers, reformers, and so forth who—like children—cannot help working, and have by their heroic efforts rediscovered the instinct of the species."

Montessori believes that if the child, the boy, the youth—at each stage of development—was given the opportunity of doing the special kind of work for which his nature craves, it would lead to a more harmonious humanity, a humanity largely delivered from the love of possession and the love of power.

There exists, in our present society, an unhappy divorce between the "working" classes and the "professional." So we have "hands" without brains, and "brains" without hands. The whole trend of Montessori's influence in the sphere of education is to unite these two elements right from the start; or better still never to allow them to be separated. As she herself says, "What God hath joined let no man put asunder!" If infants, children, and youths were trained on these practical lines at every stage of development, there would come into existence a nobler conception of work—as of something essential to the dignity of every human being.

Two Sets of Laws

Both the work of the child and that of the adult are subject to certain laws; but since (as we have seen) their work differs in nature, so do the laws which govern them.

Let us look first at the laws which govern the work of an adult.

(1) *Division of Labor.* Since the end of the adult's labor is an external one—to produce something—it is possible to divide up his work, and share it between a number of persons. "Many hands make light work." Also the work can be differentiated according to kind and quality.

(2) *"Maximum Result with Minimum Effort."* Arising out of the external nature of the adult's work comes the fact that he seeks to produce as much as he can with the least amount of effort. This does not, in itself, imply any unwillingness to work, but simply means that there exists a nice economy of effort. Hence the adult can use labor-saving devices to shorten his hours of labor.

Now when we come to look at the child's work we find that these two laws simply do not apply. If you come to think of it, there can be no no "division of labor" in his case. Since his work is, in essence, to grow, he *must* do it himself; and no one, however willing, can do it for him. In fact "every useless aid arrests development"—and "to become a man of twenty he must take twenty years."

It is the same with the second law—"maximum result with minimum effort." This, too, does not apply to the child's work, "which springs from an internal fount of energy which has no quantitative relation to the external end."

The Joy of Work

Because the child's work springs from this "internal fount of energy" it is no burden to him—any more than we feel the beating of the heart to be a burden. They are both vital functions. But the work of the child is on a higher plane than the beating of the heart—a mental plane; hence he consciously rejoices in it, "as a strong man to run a race."

Work is for him a necessary form of life, a vital instinct without which his personality cannot organize itself. So essential is it for the child to have the opportunity and means for this creative "work" that if it is denied him his deviated energies will result in all sorts of abnormalities. Conversely, there is one thing, and one only, which will cure the child of his abnormalities—and that is work. This is Dr. Montessori's doctrine of "normalization through work."

It is this joy which the children manifest in their work which makes the Montessori school so indefinably attractive. Theirs is indeed a cosmic joy, which springs from the very heart of being, because it is the joy that comes through acting in accordance with the laws of one's nature.

As soon as one understands Montessori's idea of the nature of the child's work, many mystifying phenomena become clearer. Chief among these is the well-known and remarkable tendency of children to repeat the same thing over and over again.

A two-year-old boy of my acquaintance removed and replaced the lid of the little box in which I kept my shaving soap 42 times in succession—quite spontaneously. Preyer relates how his little boy did the same thing with the stopper of a bottle 54 times. A Dutch friend of mine watched—unseen—while a little girl traced her fingers over a single sandpaper letter more than 100 times! I knew a nurse who told the same story to a little girl 25 times—at the child's own request.

What drives children to this apparently meaningless repetition? In one of her training courses Dr. Montessori forced a group of her students to repeat the exercise of taking out and replacing the wooden cylinders for 20 minutes, without stopping, till they were heartily sick of it! At the end of this she remarked with one of her illuminating smiles, "Now by the very boredom you have experienced in this repeating and repeating this same exercise, you will be able to measure that imperious inner urge that drives children to do the same thing."

At this point Montessori utters a word of practical warning to directresses. If you see this sort of spontaneous organization of work springing up in your class, beware of the temptation to systematize it. A directress might think, "Good! now we must do this systematically; make a program; draw out a timetable; make lists of children for each job, and so on." "Not" (continues the Dottoressa) "that this would be a crime, but the experienced directress —who seeks always to know the limits of her intervention—will do so here also.

"The instinct towards such organization in children is as irresistible as that which, at other times, drives them to solitary work. Even then it is not the same thing as with adults. For with the latter it is willed and rational; with children, instinctive. Their distribution of the work among themselves is not the fruit of reason, but of a harmonious cohesion which arises from that sentiment which the human instinct shows when it is about to produce its greatest work. Beware of crushing this tender thing into an adult mold. The greatest prudence is necessary, if the teacher is going to intervene, lest this graceful and charming scene should lose its character, and its light be put out."

More Exceptions That Prove the Rule

Just as there are these times when the child works like an adult towards an external end, with a minimum expenditure of effort, so there are times when the adult expends a vast amount of energy which appears to have no quantitative relationship to the outward end. Watch a man practicing his stroke at golf! He repeats the same action again and again, and yet again, producing nothing new externally. He reminds one of the child doing the cylinders, acting with the same apparently unreasonable repetition. Why does he act thus? Because his real aim—like the child's—is an internal one, to perfect himself. We might in fact apply to him, with absolute justice, the words with which Dr. Montessori describes the child at his typical work: "He wastes an immense amount of energy over an insubstantial end; and he wastes not only driving energy but intensive energy in the exact execution of every detail." ("Shoulder up!" "Keep your eye on the ball!" etc.)

If this is true of the sporting man it is even more so of the spiritual man whose aim is to advance his spiritual growth. He too makes use of external things in his environment with an internal aim—the perfection of his soul.

The Child's "Work" Is "Useless" . . .

Looked at from the point of view of the "practical" adult (whose aim is to produce something outside himself) the child's work is quite useless. The work of the adult has a social value; he produces something which is useful to society. In one of her lectures Dr. Montessori drew a striking imaginary picture of the adult workers of the world. There was the blacksmith at his anvil; the builder at his wall; the farmer at his plough; the scientist in his laboratory; the legislator with his new code of laws, and so forth. In and out among these busy workers wanders the child. But among them there is no place for him, nor his "work." He does not belong there because he is of no "use" there; he is an alien to that society of busy adult workers. He is in fact an "extra-social" being because he cannot adapt himself to the standards and aims of this adult society; and so can take no part in it.

But Not Really Useless

Nevertheless, if we look into the matter more deeply, the child's work is far from being useless. In fact, it is just as important as that of the adult—even more so. It is not we adults who can transform a child into a man, any more than we could transform a man into a baby. That is the child's work—to create the adult!

It is by virtue of the child's incessant activity, as he unconsciously carries out this great aim, that we call him a worker. For he does not "create the man" by meditation or rest, but by unceasing, unwearied activity, carried on, year in and year out, for upwards of twenty years. As Montessori says:

> The child exercises himself, moves himself, makes his own experiments, learns to coordinate his movements, goes hither and thither seizing ideas from the external world. He learns, in what seems a miraculous manner, to speak, to stand upright on his feet, to walk, to run—in all this seeking, little by little, to give precise form to his intelligence—so that we can say: these are the characteristics, and this the intelligence of a child of five, and of eight, and of eighteen respectively; for the child will not disobey the program drawn up for him by nature. Thus, through indefatigable activity, through efforts, experiments, conquests, and griefs; through harsh trials and wearisome struggles, step by step he fulfills his difficult and glorious task, adding always a new perfection.

Great and important as the child's work is, it has never yet been fully recognized by society—the chief reason being because it does not produce anything visibly useful outside itself, as is the case with adult labor.

The Two Dependencies

If the child cannot do the adult's work it is equally true that the adult cannot do the child's. The perfection of the full-grown man depends—when you come to think of it—on this long-continued work of the child who creates him. The adult, if you look at it in this way, is just as dependent on the child for the richness of his physical, mental, and spiritual endowments as the child, for his part, is dependent on the adult for his many needs. In his own sphere the child is master and can say, "I, too, have a kingdom; and you—adults—are my dependents." Upon the realization of these two dependencies, Montessori sees the only foundation on which to build "the fundamental framework for harmony among mankind."

C. Commentary and Analysis

Perhaps the most surprising impression we have when reading of the children in a Montessori school is the intense interior activity with which the child continually acts. The child's work is truly interior. It is unceasing yet never hurried, intense and somehow never tiring. The goal of the child's work is not present to him and yet his effort flows forth toward his goal irresistibly and joyfully. The facial expression of the working child manifests "the satisfaction of a profound need of life." To the child, work, play, rest, leisure are all quite naturally integrated. The spontaneity with which the child takes up an activity, the delight with which he repeats and repeats it until his organism and mind are satisfied, the remarkable creativity he displays in achieving his goal—all these are indications of a deep and beautiful process moving in a quiet but direct line. And we sense that we have merely been permitted to glimpse only the smallest vision of the whole picture.

We may not be too far off the mark in reading this phenomenon as an indication of how closely man is related to material creation.

In the development of the human person Montessori speaks of the crucial importance of what she calls "sensitive periods."

Children pass through definite periods in which they reveal psychic aptitudes and possibilities which afterward disappear. That is why, at particular epochs of their life, they reveal an intense and extraordinary interest in certain objects and exercises, which one might look for in vain at a later age. During such a period the child is endowed with a special sensibility which urges him to focus his attentions on certain aspects of his environment to the exclusion of others. Such attention is not the result of mere curiosity; it is more like a burning passion (Standing, p. 120).

The intensely long period of activity brought about and sustained by a "sensitive period" produces not fatigue but fulfillment: the child is not worn out but is stronger than before, for he is doing the work by which he "creates" himself.

Montessori discovered sensitive periods for learning language, for order, for interest in objects, for the refinement of sense powers, for learning good manners, as well as many of the sensitive periods which occur later in youth and adolescence, when there is a special interest in the intellectual, social, emotional and cultural life and a striving for new levels of personality development.

When the Christian reflects on these insights into human development, he immediately sees with what great reverence and concern the growth and education of the child must be cared for. The child's chances of living a productive life to his fullest capacities depend very heavily upon the proper development of his mental, physical and emotional powers. Despite the fact that the work of the child differs so radically from the "work" of the adult, there are very few parents or teachers who would disvalue the work of the child as it prepares him for the work of adult life. Parents in general clearly recognize their responsibilities in seeing that their children are educated in school, though at times some parents forget (or perhaps were never aware of) the less formal kinds of learning that the child needs, for example, toward a sense of order, solitude, responsibility.

When the child's organism is developing properly and according to nature, Montessori tells us that we should expect to see emerging what she calls a "normalized child." Some of the characteristics of the normalized child are: a love of order, a love of work (the child's construction of his own personality), profound spontaneous concentration, a love of silence, sublimation of the possessive instinct, a spirit of obedience within a spirit of independence and initiative, joy, creativity, a preference for mutual aid rather than competition.

How many adults would be happy to possess even a few of the qualities of the "normalized child!" Each quality is a pearl of great price, hard to find, more difficult to hold on to and preserve. For the Christian also, these qualities of the "normalized child" are the human qualities within which a fruitful life of grace will take seed and grow. Furthermore, they are the qualities so desirable in the world of work within the context of a Christian ethic. The more deeply these qualities are allowed to develop in childhood, the better chance they have of remaining as part of the grown-up's life. In any case, according to Montessori, "nature" within the human organism points quite clearly to the goals of human development as well as the qualities which should normally blossom in the human person.

Underlying the observation of the qualities of the normalized child lies an important though often unobserved fact. The source and basis of the emergence and flourishing of these qualities of order, work, concentration, creativity and the rest centers in the organism's interaction with the environment, or more simply, the human body finds itself naturally absorbed in and captivated by material creation, whether this creation be one's own body and feelings, the body and feelings of another, or individual objects in the material world. In any case, the child finds deep satisfaction in dealing with the material world; it is the field in which he grows and discovers himself.

This communication with the world in order to find himself is a motif of childhood, to know, understand and eventually transform the world about him. It would seem that a union so natural and spontaneous in the child is a strong indication that a human's love for the created world and his work in it should also be a motif of a "normalized" adult life.

In many cases, however, we grown-ups have rejected the natural love for the world around us which the child possesses. Often our work life is characterized by boredom rather than surprise. The openness to reality which is the child's we no longer possess. Often in us the hunger to create is gone. And with the natural curiosity in human life waning, our Christian enthusiasm also grows dim.

There is a great fear today of secularization, of a total absorption with the world to the exclusion of God. Perhaps the child is trying to tell us that through working in the world, in letting ourselves fall in love with the lovable creation that surrounds us, we might "discover" ourselves by responding to the earth through our senses and minds and feelings, not with that characteristically adult fear and hesitation but with the simple eager openness of the child.

The child is living proof that the created world has much to tell us, of itself, of ourselves, of God. The price of discovery, as we learn from the child, requires a concentrated effort, a desire to discover and create, a patience with details, an openness to growth and communication.

It is quite like God to communicate through the quiet activity of children at work to those who have eyes to see.

For those who have eyes to see into the future, the potentialities of Montessori's normalized child fill the Christian optimist with hope. Montessori's chief claim lies not in the fact that she has developed a new educational method, but rather in that she has discovered the characteristics of the normal child, pointing out that "given the right conditions, children change their character, almost their nature, revealing profound qualities in the infant soul which had hitherto remained unknown." Furthermore, she learned these laws and identified the sensitive periods from observing the children themselves.

Such normalized children, says E. M. Standing, "have indeed inspired a new hope for the future of humanity," by liberating psychic energies which lay unnoticed and undeveloped before this. For Christian thinkers like Teilhard de Chardin who see the world becoming more "one" and approaching through the work of modern science and human understanding closer and closer to the kingdom, such programs and insights like Montessori's give promise to a solidly founded hope for a full flowering of human potential among individuals and communities on all dimensions of life.

Questions for Discussion

1. What are the fundamental differences between the work of the adult and the work of the child?
2. What are the laws which govern the work of the adult? Are these laws relevant to the work of the child? Explain.
3. Is the child's work "useless" or not? Discuss.
4. What is meant by "sensitive periods"? What are some of the characteristics of the "normalized child"?
5. Indicate some of the insights yielded by a Christian reflection on the discoveries of Maria Montessori.

V
THE WORKER
AND HIS EDUCATION

A. Prenote

Both formal education and informal education in the United States develop in young men and women a certain strong orientation to work and the world of work. With the cultural value placed upon occupation and status in our society, a technological-age education naturally becomes a more and more powerful vehicle in forming and reforming man's image and value of himself.

Historically, there was a time when leisure and not work was the maker of the gentleman. Today work is everyone's responsibility, work is universal. Modern technology has reinforced the democratization of society and therefore the growth of democratic education. Hence, as the nature of occupations becomes increasingly complex and more intellectual, the requirements of the level of attainment and duration of education become a dominant consideration for life itself, thus also for Christian life.

The close interrelation between education and work in our society is obvious. An individual works to achieve the goals he chooses for himself, goals he most likely discovered and became acquainted with during his formal education. In *Education and the Common Good* Philip Phenix states:

> In the success-oriented society, education is completely vocationalized. All teaching and learning are justified in the light of their contribution to work. Education is the key to social mobility, via the ladder of social achievement (p. 95).

From the viewpoint of formal education, Dr. James W. Trent and his colleagues, Irene J. Athey and Judith L. Craise, discuss in the selection excerpted below the influence of work-careers upon education and the directions of change in educational modes demanded by the changing world of work. Dr. Trent is codirector and assistant research psychologist of the High School Graduate Study, Center for the Study of Higher Education, University of California, Berkeley. The article was originally published in *Educational Record* 46 (1965), pp. 93-103.

B. Selection: Technology, Education and Human Development

A primary objective of college educators and of counselors is the guidance of youth toward self-fulfillment and effective living. But since this responsibility must be carried out within the framework of conditions imposed by a rapidly changing technological society, the objective of education will remain vague unless a better understanding of the nature of society and sounder criteria for effective living are established. If educators are to prepare America's youth to assume adequate adult roles in society, then the nature of society must be carefully examined. This procedure is crucial because it provides the backdrop against which educators must evaluate and try to enhance the effectiveness of their educational enterprises.

In assessing the nature of society, it will not do to base judgments on the world as it has appeared in the past, nor even as it appears today. Society is now in the throes of a second industrial revolution whose magnitude already far exceeds its predecessor. To meet the resulting challenges, it will no longer be appropriate to think and educate in terms of an outmoded industrial society. Even now, modern technological society is in a continuous process of change. Therefore it may be necessary to assist our youth to develop new and flexible approaches to living in a social environment where the population is already in need of education in skills radically different from those formerly required.

That the nation as a whole has become increasingly aware of the need for more education may be reflected in the surging rise of college enrollments. However, accompanying this growing awareness among many laymen is a tacit assumption that more education is the touchstone that will eliminate employment problems and lead to universal prosperity. A recent article in a popular magazine commending "instant education" is a case in point.[1] Those who have not previously attended college are prone to see it as an "instant" panacea for all social ills. However, a number of thoughtful critics have been more realistic about the problems and limitations of formal education, even while redefining education as the new religion of society.[2] In fact, it may be argued that a blind belief in education *per se* may make it an outmoded, ritualized induction into society that will only produce stereotypic modes of thinking and an inability to comprehend the real problems at hand.

Consequently, the argument presented here is that more education is desirable, but that it should be geared toward greater human development. As one concerned scientist has pointed out, our "democratic-scientific society" depends upon "the full range of human wisdom" and therefore cannot "evolve constructively without a wide endowment among its people of art, music, history, literature, and social dynamics."[3] It follows that the kind and quality of education needed for the development of the full range of human wisdom requires increased review and revision of a type that is apparent now in many quarters. This is particularly apparent in the face of the vast changes in society that automation is effecting.

As a result, educational revision might well be supplemented by a greater understanding of the present status of both the educa-

---

[1] T. George Harris, "Automation: We Can Handle It," *Look* (Jan. 12, 1965), pp. 58-62.

[2] John Hannaford, "The Coming Redefinition of Higher Education," address presented to the annual meeting of the Indiana College Personnel Association, Nov. 6, 1964.

[3] Glenn Seaborg, "A Scientific Society—The Beginnings," *Science* (Feb. 16, 1962), p. 508.

tional and employment patterns upon which automation and cybernation may have a bearing. As a starting point for thinking about the impact of cybernation and its educational implications, a few salient points put forward by Theobald may suffice to clarify the arguments of this paper: the net growth of the labor force is expected to increase greatly in this decade while, conversely, job opportunities are expected to decline rapidly with expanded automation. Large numbers of youth, particularly those with inadequate education, cannot in the near future expect to hold market-supported jobs as we understand them today. Lower levels of management may be expected to be displaced since decision-making will no longer be necessary at these levels. Indeed, only a small percentage of the population may be expected to produce all the goods needed for society's maintenance.

The exact impact of automation remains problematical, but if Theobald's account only approximates reality, the implications are awesome. To expand some of the implications of Theobald's points, a number of far-reaching and profound changes appear likely to occur. New systems of income distribution may be required to ensure that everyone is provided with the basic necessities. These economic changes may meet considerable resistance, especially from the established middle class. They may also necessitate the instigation of meaningful activity designed to promote the fullest possible development of the individual's intellectual potential and personality, regardless of whether he is gainfully employed in the manner of the past. Previously, the main outlet for a man's sense of self-satisfaction and the respect of the other members of his society has been through work. In the future, that primary outlet may be severely limited. This situation may call for new concepts and attitudes regarding work and the use of leisure if the individual is to maintain a sense of pride and worth in what he is doing. In addition, skills requisite to the implementation of complex decisions made with knowledge, wisdom, and freedom from partisan pressures may be imperative if justice and individual liberty are to be maintained and if economic chaos and international disaster are to be avoided—particularly in view of the interwoven network of national and international affairs. A liberal education may be equally essential for all, if unlimited leisure is to lead to creative human development and social productivity rather than stagnation and discontent.

Therefore, education of an exceptionally high quality will be needed at all levels, not only to provide training in specialized technical skills but also to promote a broad knowledge of and interest in human affairs. First, however, many people must be motivated to take advantage of the existing educational opportunities open to them. This problem, which currently faces teachers in depressed areas, is likely to become more extensive as unemployment spreads to the higher echelons of the industrial society. For some time the task of bringing education and enlightenment to children who have never been imbued with the desire to learn or discover for themselves has been particularly burdensome. And even those who have obtained an extensive education, but whose educational objectives have been primarily social prestige or monetary success, may also need assistance in making major shifts in their value systems—particularly if changes in society demand a reorientation which the individual cannot make unaided.

At the same time, it may not be categorically assumed that the population is entirely unable to cope with its changing environment without special assistance or that any one method is essential in dealing with the environment. Particular care must be taken by educators and other leaders not to suppress individual freedom by arbitrarily imposing their own values on students or subordinates. For example, the personality traits deemed important by the authors for effective living in the future must be regarded as their opinion, to be distinguished from the empirical data presented. The acquisition of attributes of flexibility and intellectual interests may be necessary for the individual in assuming a suitable role for himself in the future. Others might argue, however, that these traits may breed dissatisfaction, or be impossible to obtain for most individuals; or that the individual may automatically adapt to environment changes. Therefore, the problem before us may be seen as a need to seek out methods of social training or guidance without resorting to manipulative social engineering which would restrict the autonomy of the individual.

To meet this challenge, college educators need not only an

over-all picture of national patterns of college attendance, but
also insight into students' background characteristics and motivations associated with variations in these patterns or with complete rejection of educational opportunity. With such knowledge,
college educators may have a more solid and practical basis for
"retooling" their educational enterprises in order to provide best
for the needs of the new age.

The High School Graduate Study

In this context, findings are reported from a longitudinal five-
year study, conducted at the Center for the Study of Higher Education, University of California, Berkeley. The High School Graduate
Study was designed to investigate the general intellectual and non-
intellectual development of 10,000 high school graduates in six-
teen communities across the United States. Just prior to high
school graduation, information was obtained from the graduates
regarding their personality characteristics; values; goals; academic
aptitudes; and social, economic, educational, and cultural backgrounds. Data concerning the subsequent careers of all graduates
in the fall of 1959 were also collected.

Through the cooperation of the colleges entered by these graduates, complete records of their performance were obtained for the
four years following high school. Information concerning the vocational and educational experiences of the graduates who did not
enter college was gathered at intervals. Follow-up information of
this kind was obtained through 1962 from over 90 percent
of the basic sample. Modified versions of the original 1959 questionnaire and personality inventory were administered a second
time to both groups in the spring of 1963. Complete data for ap-
proximately half the original sample and about 70 percent of the
continuing college sample were obtained, supplemented by personal interviews of a representation of the entire sample.

Factors Affecting College Attendance

Of the 10,000 graduates who comprised the basic sample, 40
percent entered college full time the semester following graduation. The highest entrance rate was found in communities with
junior colleges. Communities with extension centers possessed

the lowest rate of college attendance, as low as communities with no college at all. Ability is seen to be definitely related to college attendance, but at the same time a wide diversity of ability is apparent among students entering college. Perhaps even more important is the fact that a very large proportion of the sample's brightest students did *not* enter college.

Socioeconomic status, like ability, is closely associated with educational status. Three out of every four students from professional families entered college in 1959, compared to only one in four from homes of semiskilled and unskilled workers. Of interest is the fact that, when holding first ability, and then socioeconomic status, constant, social status was found to have more bearing on college attendance than academic ability.

Factors Related to Progress in College

Sex, religion, personality disposition, family relationships, and motivation all have a bearing on educational pursuits and progress. All these factors appear interrelated, but also distinct from one another. Consequently the function of only a few of these variables will be summarized in order to illustrate how they distinguish those who persisted in college for four years compared to those who withdrew and also those high school graduates of high ability who did not attend college.

In this case the bright noncollege students are defined as those in the uppermost 30 percent of the sample's ability distribution who did not attend college during the four years subsequent to high school graduation. Those who remained in college consistently during the four years following their high school graduation are termed "persisters." The persisters comprised students who completed their degree requirements by 1963 ("completers") and those who continued their undergraduate work beyond 1963 ("continuers"). All findings are based on questionnaire returns from the 1963 follow-up sample.

Parents' temperaments (as perceived by the subjects) and their interest in and encouragement of their children were paramount among the complex of familial factors which clearly distinguished the various student groups. College persisters more frequently than any of the older student groups described their parents as loving, energetic, and ambitious. In contrast, the bright nonattenders considered their parents to be more indifferent toward their achievements and much less often a ready source of advice and consultation compared to the persisters. In addition to this kind of family support and encouragement, before graduating from high school 70 percent of the college persisters stated that their parents definitely wanted them to attend college, compared to 48 percent of the dropouts and only 15 percent of the bright nonattenders.

These data suggest that family climate is related to academic motivation, an important finding inasmuch as degree of persistence was differentiated by various aspects of motivation. Academic motivation appeared not only to be related to the ability and socioeconomic status of the students, but also to exist independently of these other factors. For example, as many students who completed college mentioned financial and academic difficulties as did the dropout students. Moreover, a large number of dropout students and, by definition, all bright nonattenders were rated in the uppermost 30 percent of the sample's ability distribution, indicating that ability alone could not account for the differences in motivation found among the groups.

The motivational factors distinguishing these different groups seem crucial since the persisters showed greater staying power while experiencing similar academic and economic difficulties and possessing the same level of ability as the other groups. It appears that what is in part related to their different achievements is the greater emphasis and value they placed on the college experience itself. The following are among the motivational and value factors differentiating persisters in college from dropout students and, to an even greater degree, from bright nonattenders: a great liking of high school; an earlier decision to attend college (though it might well be noted that the vast majority of all students made the decision whether or not to attend college before entering their junior year of high school); greater assurance expressed in 1959 that they would complete their college education; greater stress placed on the purpose of education as the gaining of knowledge and ideas rather than vocational skills; longer hours of study, regardless of hours spent in gainful employment; and more frequent use of both academic and vocational counseling.

An individual's motivations, including academic motivations, are closely related to his values and attitudes. Out of the many attitudinal traits found to differentiate the various groups, the most important were personal autonomy and intellectual disposition. The autonomy scale is a major measure of authoritarianism; it indicates the extent to which a person can think independently and objectively without reliance upon stereotyping or unquestioning dependence upon higher authority. It measures also a person's openness to and tolerance for other people and their ideas.

The vast majority of the persisting students obtained an autonomy score which exceeded the average score obtained by the dropouts and bright nonattenders. Autonomy, perhaps more than any other trait, distinguishes the college completer from the dropout, and the dropout, in turn, from the bright nonattender. The large mean differences between these groups suggest that a disproportionate amount of authoritarianism is exhibited by the college dropouts and nonattenders; these groups rank considerably lower than the completers in the degree of flexibility, openness, and objectivity they exhibit in their thinking as measured by the autonomy scale.

Autonomy is related to intellectual disposition, and this trait, too, clearly distinguishes the groups. Intellectual disposition in the study was assessed by combining scores on several attitudinal scales which measure a person's inclination toward reflective, abstract thinking, intellectual curiosity, tolerance for ambiguity, and artistic interests.

Less than 20 percent of the students in the sample who entered college were at the high intellectuality level. Differences in intellectuality between the college completers and continuing students are noteworthy; even more remarkable are the differences between the persisting students and the dropouts and nonattenders.

PERCENTAGE OF STUDENTS GROUPED BY COLLEGE EXPERIENCE
AT EACH LEVEL OF INTELLECTUAL DISPOSITION

		LEVEL OF INTELLECTUAL DISPOSITION		
COLLEGE GROUPS	No.	High (%)	Middle (%)	Low (%)
Completers....................	777	21	40	39
Continuers....................	523	19	30	51
Dropouts........................	873	10	28	62
Bright nonattenders........	504	4	20	76

These data appear to have an important bearing upon the considerations put forward at the beginning of this paper. By way of judging the possible social significance of the data, certain questionnaire responses which varied by level of intellectuality were observed. Some of the responses (and there were many) that distinguished the high from low intellectuality level students, usually by at least 25 percent, were:

1. The belief that the major purpose of education is the gaining of ideas and creative development rather than vocational training.

2. Making the decision to attend college as early as elementary school.

3. Plans to attend graduate school.

4. Dissatisfaction with rules and regulations that are too rigid, unpermissive, and fail to promote self-responsibility.

5. The belief that justice and understanding among men is a major issue facing mankind.

The data just cited substantiate the view that level of intellectuality is directly related to creative, flexible thinking, interest in new ideas, educational aspirations, degrees of self-direction, and concern about the issues facing mankind. If these traits may be regarded as aspects of human development needed for the new society, as we suggested in the opening thesis of this paper, then it seems significant that the manifestation of these traits differentiates students who succeed in college from those who either fail to attend or withdraw prematurely.

At the same time there is not observable any great development of intellectual disposition over a span of four years, whatever the group differences. This may be occasioned by the formation of basic values such as intellectual disposition in the earliest years of life. This phenomenon is suggested in the above data by the early decision to attend college reported by the high school graduates, and the apparent effect of parental values on this decision. The implication is that the fostering of intellectual attitudes and academic motivation must begin much earlier than the senior year in high school if it is desirable to promote a different orientation for the individual in order to assist him toward greater intellectual and social growth. The data also give some idea of the importance of the role played by parents in inculcating these attitudes. The values predominant in the home environment are undoubtedly an early and major determining factor in the development of the individual's values, attitudes, and life style.

But the school shares this responsibility, since teachers, as well as parents, are among the early adult models with whom children identify. Of course, teachers can act as negative as well as positive models.[4] It is, therefore, important that teachers in the school system be dedicated to intellectual pursuits and a desire for knowledge for its own sake in order for the same values to be transmitted to their students.

A desire for increased understanding of human nature and concerns may also be important among society's technologists. Their role may not be to act as models or educators of youth, but theirs is the responsibility for the maintenance and change of much of the technical and economic systems of society providing the environment in which the human must exist. The decisions of technologists frequently affect the way of life for other members of society. It seems, therefore, almost imperative to have a knowledge of the values of these key members of society. Because the college sample contained many prospective teachers and technologists, a great deal of pertinent data was obtained which made it possible to compare these two major groups of pre-professionals with each other and with college students majoring in other fields.

---

[4] See Joseph Adelson, "The Teacher as a Model," in Nevitt Sanford, ed., *The American College* (New York: Wiley, 1962), pp. 396-417.

Disposition of Students in Various Curricula

The teacher trainees were divided into two groups, those who were pursuing concurrently a liberal arts course and a teaching credential and those who were majoring in education.

Consistently the liberal arts students appeared more intellectually oriented than the education majors. Combining percentages, only about 10 percent of the education majors were at the high intellectuality level, compared to almost 30 percent of the liberal arts groups. Fifty-five percent of the education majors were at the low level of intellectual disposition, compared to just over a third of the liberal arts students. Given this intellectual disparity, what follows is almost inevitable: the education majors were—and very significantly so:

1. The least interested in education for the sake of knowledge, ideas, and creative development.

2. The least sympathetic toward literary and artistic movements (only 10 percent showed any great sympathy toward these cultural movements compared to over 25 percent of the liberal arts students, and this small percentage of the liberal arts students is itself not very high).

3. The least prone toward browsing in a bookstore or attending a cultural event.

4. The least knowledgeable about eminent figures in the cultural world.

5. The least concerned about human relations and justice.*

In addition, the education majors were more interested in the security of steady employment than the use of their talents, and almost half of the education majors preferred homemaking or some other occupation to a career in teaching.

Some of the intellectual differences found are undoubtedly a function of socioeconomic status. But preliminary analyses suggest that a restricted economic background alone does not account for the education majors' relative lack of flexible, intellectual, and humanitarian interests. This finding seems important since these are the individuals who may soon be in a position to affect the educational and economic systems of society. A positive note in this

---

* Note: Business and engineering majors have similar attitudes (L.S.).

context, however, is that, although the group is small, the liberal arts—credential students did show themselves to be at least as intellectually oriented as other liberal arts students.

Summary and Implications

Certain dominant tendencies are suggested by the above data:

1. A very large proportion of able youth are not attending college or are withdrawing from college without completing their education.

2. Although college attendance and performance appear to be a matter of native ability, socioeconomic background and community educational opportunities, other factors, singly and interdependently associated with college attendance, are: (a) students' perception of their parents as emotionally supportive, alert, and interested in their children's progress; (b) a view of education as worthwhile in itself more than as utilitarian vocational training; (c) academic motivations; (d) personal autonomy and nonauthoritarianism; and (e) intellectual disposition.

3. Academic interest and motivation, instilled early in life, are related to college entrance and persistence, together with and independent of ability and socioeconomic status. Academic motivation and educational attainment are related to human development in terms of a flexible and intellectual disposition. But in any event few students appear to attain a high level of development as defined in this context.

4. The degree of intellectual and human development manifest among young adults varies with degree of motivation to enter and persist in college. The least flexible, objective, tolerant, and intellectually disposed students are found among bright high school graduates not attending college, students majoring in education and such fields as business and engineering, and dropout students, in that order.

These findings suggest a number of implications. Of particular interest is the bearing they have on the role of education in reference to the needs of tomorrow's society. The thesis of the present article is that, to function effectively, tomorrow's society will be highly dependent on an enlarged proportion of flexible, creative individuals whose human and intellectual potential has been as fully developed as possible; and it has been observed that the educational system will have to assume a primary responsibility for implementing this human development. But this implementation is far from being accomplished, if the data just observed are representative of the situation at large. Educational opportunity is not yet equalized in the form of community facilities, social environment, or family climate. Large numbers of society's ablest youth place little or no value on higher education and demonstrate few signs of intellectual or innovative behavior. Still larger numbers of youth forfeit the completion of their education, and even those students who do complete their college education exhibit little of the intellectual development that may be required in the new age. Perhaps the most significant of all the findings is that many teachers and technologists — those who will be most responsible for preparing the coming generation for and implementing tomorrow's changes — show the least flexibility, interest in justice and understanding among mankind, and general development of all the college students under observation.

Apparently these attributes of creativity, flexibility, and intellectuality are not being, or cannot be, developed in our colleges at the present time. Solutions to this problem are not ready-made; only a few general possibilities will be mentioned here, and they are largely based on the authors' opinions of what may constitute the good and worthwhile for society.

1. A great deal more experimentation seems necessary at all levels of education, in order to learn the most effective ways of bringing about human development for the greatest number of people. This experimentation and innovation, though currently under the auspices of colleges and universities, might well go beyond the confines of the campus and include the entire community. Perhaps much experimentation should be undertaken on the assumption that a college education as it is now known may be no solution at all, or at least no solution for many people. But what seems especially important is that such experimentation be concerned with bold new ideas, and with new methods of promoting the intellectual concerns, cultural values, and creative traits characteristic of an educated, thinking society.

2. Somehow, expanded efforts must be made to reach the many

who could profit from further education. A way must be found to identify students' potential in their earliest years so that they may be helped to develop their talents. The data above substantiate the view that, in evaluating the effectiveness of collegiate enterprises, not only questions of opportunity are involved, but also personal values and motivations — values and motivations formed long before college, but very apparent in reference to the decision to attend college and subsequent academic success. The values predominant in the home environment are undoubtedly a major factor contributing to the child's intellectual growth and his ability to deal effectively with his familial and extrafamilial environment throughout the crucial formative periods. College should continue to foster the growth of this disposition, but it can do little if this disposition has not been developed *before* college, and even before elementary school.

3. Apparently, particular attention needs to be given to the recruitment and education of teachers and technologists. Many of these professionals are not equipped with the benefits of a liberal education and do not show a humanistic value system or a desire to foster intellectual growth. Rather, they appear to be the least prepared to carry out their social responsibilities and cope with the expected repercussions of the new age. Perhaps the very best teachers should be placed in charge of the earliest elementary years, when attitudes and values are still being developed. Technologists, in turn, might well be given an enriched education in the humanities and social sciences in addition to their applied training.

A number of ongoing efforts to provide enriched educational opportunities for teachers and technologists as intended in this context can be cited. What is important is that these examples not be allowed to remain isolated occurrences in selected regions or institutions.

All of these suggested activities assume, of course, that it is in part the role of the school to transmit and develop what is inherited and is to be valued by society. But surely there appears to be no question about the necessity of inculcating the values essential to society, or the responsibility of the educational system to do so. There remains only the continual search for what constitutes an essential value, its cultivation, and its transmission without transgression upon or manipulation of the individual. Such an objective, without doubt, represents a very large order. And yet, if efforts and talents along the lines suggested above are combined, perhaps a force can be fashioned out of our educational enterprises that will enable society not only to cope with the challenges of tomorrow, but to make of tomorrow a richer, fuller life than is now known.

C. Commentary and Analysis

Today is an age of personalism as well as one of impersonalism. There is a striving for productive efficiency through standardization; yet individual human beings hunger for uniqueness. Psychologists of personality compose lists of the "characteristics of maturity." Psychologists of religion follow their colleagues in characterizing the mature religious personality. Both agree that there are certain qualities which are helpful and often necessary in order to live a full human and Christian life. By the same token there are personal and intellectual qualities which are beneficial and necessary for the Christian in his work in the world.

In the selection for this chapter we looked with Trent and his co-authors into the data of a contemporary study of students in college and their careers. According to Trent, we in America seem to be in a stage of transition regarding the human and technical qualities which will most help and influence today's technological world of work.

If the intellectual world as a whole is presently in an unsettled state, it is not surprising that the Christian faces his work in the secularized world with something less than complete assurance of what his place is and where he is going. His Christian reflection, therefore, must proceed slowly. He must carefully and profitably examine the trends and directions which humanity seems to be following as well as the discoveries which come to light through educational and motivational research. Throughout the scientific world there are individuals and teams involved in studying many of mankind's problems. The findings and inferences of such studies are important to the Christian, since they will be fundamental to the personality characteristics important for effective living in the world.

For example, a committed Christian in his work in the world is going to be most inventive and productive if he is as humanly prepared as possible to face the world. In the previous chapter we saw the importance of the qualities of the normalized child for a full adult life. In this chapter from his research Dr. Trent predicts the characteristics of the most desirable personality in the coming years, from the viewpoint of education and career-employment. He states:

> The thesis of the present article is that to function effectively, tomorrow's society will be highly dependent on an enlarged proportion of flexible, creative individuals whose human and intellectual potential has been as fully developed as possible; and it has been observed that the educational system will have to assume a primary responsibility for implementing this human development.

Educationists aware of the challenge of the second industrial revolution brought about mainly by automation are attempting to retool their educational enterprises and provide for the needs of the new age by studying student backgrounds, characteristics and motivations in relation to educational opportunities. It is hoped that by uncovering the personality traits which are important for effective living in the future, guidance counselors can better advise students regarding their career choices and future education. Some of the conclusions which emerge from Trent's study and have a special bearing on the Christian and his world of work are the following.

First of all Trent's research findings seem to indicate that intellectual values and favorable dispositions toward intellectual things are formed in the earliest years of life. The value of proper and full development of the child is once again reemphasized, as well as parental and family influence in attitudes toward education and career-choice. Similarly, the Christian's responsibility in this regard is reasserted, and the connections of this chapter with the earlier chapters on the family and the child are obvious.

Second, regarding the attitudes and qualities of today's successful college student, Trent says that the "level of intellectuality is directly related to creative, flexible thinking, interest in new ideas, educational aspirations, degrees of self-expression and concern about the issues facing mankind." The trend here which the Christian notices is the strong desire on the part of young people for creative advances, not only for their individual selves and their community but for humanity as well.

Third, Trent noted among society's scientists the desire for increased understanding of human nature and the concerns of mankind. This is one manifestation of a current trend of the integration of knowledge, which appears in academic circles in the ever-growing amount of interdisciplinary research and teaching and which manifests itself also among individuals who look to the unification of their life in all its phases, both personal and productive. This trend clearly has a strong effect on the world of work, for the complexity of life in contemporary society presents many difficulties to this integration process. To the present date, there have been very few Christian thinkers who have attempted to find a Christian synthesis such as the one which Trent is pointing to. There are certainly many Christians, especially among the scientific community, who experience painfully the problems of a compartmentalized kind of existence and seek a Christian synthesis or framework within which they could integrate their lives. The situation here is one of Christian challenge.

Fourth, education theorists who recognize that the main outlet for a man's sense of self-satisfaction and respect in society had been acquired by him through work and his work life also recognize that the change in the meaning of work now beginning to occur will demand "new concepts and attitudes regarding work and the use of leisure" if the individual is to maintain a sense of pride and personal worth in what he is doing. Naturally, it becomes the responsibility of the Christian to re-evaluate the meaning and significance of his daily work in his Christian life in the world today.

For example, Dr. Trent claims that "a liberal education may be equally essential for all, if unlimited leisure is to lead to creative human development and social productivity rather than stagnation and discontent." Furthermore, the challenge mankind faces implies education of an exceptionally high quality at all levels both in specialized technical skills and in those branches which "promote a broad knowledge of and interest in human affairs."

The phenomenon of education on higher and higher levels reaching more and more people is not a panacea for the problems of the new society. It creates other problems. For example, the gap growing between those who have obtained an extensive education and those who cannot or refuse to take advantage of available educational opportunities, is becoming quite burdensome.

More specifically, interdisciplinary activity occurring in centers of learning is naturally carried on at what might be called a highbrow intellectual level of communication. Each of the scientific disciplines has its own technical language, or jargon, which only the initiates of the particular science understand. For those who can understand, the technical language is an invaluable tool and probably itself accounts for much of the rapid progress which the sciences are experiencing. However, the jargon, such as is found in the textbooks and journals of the psychologist and sociologist, while it serves to speed up communication among the scientists themselves, often effectively widens the communication gap between the social scientist and the man in the street. At times the layman in the scientific world feels that he understands some idea or concept of, let us say, the psychologist, yet he is really far from the mark. Such misunderstanding is likely only to distort attempts at further communication. It is not surprising to learn that in some instances research scientists communicate only with one another, within a small community of initiates.

When the topic of concern is theology and the Christian life, we must admit that there are too few writers among professional theologians who can communicate their insights and conclusions to the ordinary Christian. It is not that such men prefer to live intellectually in a current different from that of the rest of the Christian community. Rather it is simply that specialized education once again has created a chasm between the theologian and the man in the pew: the layman cannot understand the technical jargon and the theologian is often without the capacity or the time to translate his specialized language into terms common to both himself and the layman. There is a great need for communication between the theologian and the other members of the Christian community.

Questions for Discussion

1. Why is an understanding of a changing technological society necessary for effective education? What will be the most significant future effect of cybernation upon the individual and his relation to work? What does this imply for education?
2. What aspects of family climate are most related to academic motivation? What are the motivational and value factors which distinguish "persisters" in college from dropouts? What two attitudinal traits of the individual are most significant in this connection? What further traits distinguish between high and low intellectuality levels among students?
3. When are basic values such as intellectual disposition formed? What is the implication of this? In the college sample studied, what were some of the significant characteristics of education majors? What bearing does this have on the needs of tomorrow's society?
4. What is the thesis of the article by Trent and his colleagues? What directions does the study propose for future educational preparation?
5. Indicate some of the ways the study's conclusions affect the problem of the Christian in his world of work. What further problems remain?

VI
THE WORKER
AND HIS CULTURE

A. Prenote

So far we have studied the meaning of work from the viewpoint of the sociologist, the psychologist and the educator. In this chapter we look at work through the eyes of the cultural anthropologist.

From his analysis of different cultures, the anthropologist realizes that the intense interrelation of work, education, status, success, and many other variables is based upon the deep strands of shared values which underlie our society and weave the strong but pliable fabric of our cultural life.

A culture may be defined as a *system of shared habits*. The important point is that culture is the product of learning, not heredity; it uses the same learning mechanisms as those involved in habit formation. Descriptions of cultures are therefore a reconstruction of the collective habits and customs which underlie actual social behavior.

With Cora Du Bois' article, presented in this chapter, we gain an anthropological insight into the fundamental system of cultural values prominent in the American society — the values which seem to have been most continually influential in shaping the attitudes of Americans for the past 300 years.

In her value profile of American culture Dr. Du Bois isolates three focal values, *material well-being, conformity,* and *effort-optimism,* which help to explain much of the behavior of individuals living in our society. The effort-optimism value refers to work, which is valued in our society even for itself. That is, it is a *good thing* simply to have something to do, something with which to keep busy. When in addition the outcome of the human effort is successful, the cultural value is further strengthened. The connection of these three focal values with the meaning of work, its influence on our lives and the problems it begets will become self-evident. The article by Dr. Du Bois which follows is taken from *American Anthropologist* 57 (1955), pp. 1232-1239.

B. Selection: The Dominant Value Profile of American Culture

This paper is an attempt to synthesize and systematize the revelant insights on American values advanced by a diverse group of writers from De Tocqueville through Myrdal to the authors of the polemic or conversational pieces that have been so numerous in the last decade. It will be addressed to the dominant value system of middle-class Americans. This system is rooted in the Protestant ethic and eighteenth-century rationalism. Many of its specific values are shared with other societies, but its configuration has come to be considered peculiarly American.

Since the allotted space is limited, what is said here must be condensed, schematic, and highly selective. There is no attempt to give a new definition of value or to adhere rigidly to existing ones. Distinctions between value and related concepts like themes, configurations, etc., will not be argued. Furthermore, the comments made here do not stem from scientific investigations. Readers interested in the attempt of anthropologists to grapple with such subtle and difficult questions are referred to more competent and exhaustive materials.[1] Dr. Ethel Albert's still unpublished material furnishes whatever logical coherence this paper may have,

---

[1] Cf., eg., Clyde Kluckhohn, et al., "Value and Value Orientation in the Theory of Action," in Talcott Parsons and Edward A. Shils, eds., *Toward a General Theory of Action* (Cambridge, Mass.: Harvard University Press, 1951), pp. 388-433; also, Florence Kluckhohn, "Dominant and Substitute Profiles of Cultural Orientations: Their Significance for the Analysis of Social Stratification," *Social Forces* 28 (1950), pp. 376-93.

but for the content and interpretations the writer must assume full responsibility.

The Oppositional Mode

Oppositional propositions are a consistent aspect of Western European culture. They represent recurrent dilemmas in logic and ethics. They are reflected in, and fostered by, the structure of Indo-European languages. They have permeated sociological and psychological conceptualization. A wide range of oppositional propositions can be offered as illustrations: thesis-antithesis; good-evil; subject-predicate; folk-urban; aggression-submission; superordinate-subordinate; mind-body. Of these oppositional propositions some may be genuine in the sense that they are, logically speaking, contraries. But it seems probable that most oppositional propositions current in Western culture are preponderantly spurious in the sense that they are poorly conceived contradictories.

The assumption is made here that no system of values can encompass genuine contraries and therefore that the oppositional propositions in any value system are spurious. The further assumption is made that in any value system where such spurious oppositions exist there will be a strain for consistency.

The implication of these assumptions for the processes of value change are clear. Analytically, any attempt to present a value system should avoid the formulation of new and spurious oppositions. The avoidance of analytic oppositions may help to reveal those already extant in the existing value system, and the associated strains for consistency may emerge more clearly.

The strain for consistency in the American value system may be one of the forces accounting for changes in its configuration over the last three hundred years. Whether that strain is more intense in the American value system than in others it is impossible to estimate here. However, that the strain exists has been manifest in two major directions: (1) the prizing of change itself, usually expressed as effort, struggle, and progress, which will be discussed again in connection with the focal value called "effort-optimism," and (2) compromise, which is not exclusively American but has received characteristic expression in the phrase "splitting the difference." This phrase reveals particularly an appreciation of the spurious quality of the oppositions, since it implies that neither oppositional term represents "truth" and that by retreating from false dichotomies a valid equilibrium may be achieved.

Four Basic Premises

For our purposes the value premises of any culture can be considered to rest upon the assumptions made concerning man's cognitive view of the universe, man's relation to it, and man's relation to other men. For the American middle class it is postulated that: (1) the universe is mechanistically conceived, (2) man is its master, (3) men are equal, and (4) men are perfectible. From these four basic premises alone many of the focal and specific values, as well as the directives, of the American value system can be derived. In the context of the last three hundred years of American history these assumptions have proved valid both experientially and integratively (i.e., in a self-reinforcing sense) for the United States as a whole and, more specifically, for the American middle class. Despite changed situations and therefore the potential loss of experiential and integrative validation, we may nevertheless expect these assumptions to persist for a considerable period of time. There may be lags in a value system as there are in other aspects of culture.

Focal Values and Their Directives

Albert uses the term "focal" to designate a value about which numerous specific values cluster. Directives are used to designate the do's and dont's inherent in specific as well as focal values.[2]

The four premises given above yield at least three major focal values: material well-being that derives from the premise that man is master of a mechanistic universe; conformity that derives from the premise of man's equality; effort-optimism that derives from the premise of man's perfectibility. (The fortunate term "effort-optimism" was coined by the Kluckhohns.)[3]

---

[2] Ethel M. Albert, "Theory Construction for the Comparative Study of Values in Five Cultures: A Report on the Value Study," 1954, pp. 22-23 [dittoed], Harvard University: Laboratory of Social Relations.

[3] Clyde and Florence Kluckhohn, "American Culture: Generalized Orientations and Class Patterns," in Lyman Bronson, ed., *Conflicts of Power in*

The nexus of specific values and directives clustering around each of these focal values can now be considered. Simultaneously the mutual reinforcement that occurs between the basic premises and their focal values, as well as the constant effort to resolve spurious oppositions through change, can be underlined. The inner consistency of the value system here presented accounts for much of the traditional vigor of "the American way of life" in the past. However, such vigor could not have existed without the reinforcement provided by the geographic setting of the American nation and the historic forces operative in the broader setting of Western European commercial, industrial, technical, and scientific growth in which the American nation shared.

1. *Effort-Optimism*

Work is a specific value in American society. It is not so much a necessary condition of existence as a positive good. It is a specific instrumental value through which man strives to reach not only the goal of his own perfectibility but also the goal of mastering a mechanistically conceived universe. But in values Vaihinger's "law of the preponderance of the means over the ends" is frequently operative. Thus work becomes a goal in itself and in the process may acquire the quality of activity for its own sake. Thus recreation, although theoretically the antithesis of work, nevertheless in its activism shows many of the aspects of work. "Fun" is something that most Americans work hard for and at, so that they must be warned at forty to give up tennis for golf, or hunting trips for painting. Touring, whether at home or abroad, acquires the quality of a marathon. And this in turn is closely associated with another specific value linked with the effort-optimism syndrome, the importance placed on education. However, as we shall see later, the educational effort acquires a particularly American cast when taken in conjunction with the other two focal values, material well-being and conformity. In sum, as many foreigners have observed, American life gives the impression of activism. The directives, as well as the virtues and vices, associated with this optimistic activism are

Modern Culture: Seventh Symposium (New York: [Conference on Science, Philosophy and Religion in Their Relation to the Democratic Way of Life, Inc.] Harper [distributors], 1947).

numerous: "If at first you don't succeed, try, try again"; or, in the more contemporary idiom, "Let's get this show on the road." The optimistic quality that pervades the American mood is clearly conveyed by the "bigger ergo better" mentality; the "never say die"; the "up and at 'em."

Vigor, at least as motility, connotes biologic youth. The cult of youthfulness in this society is again a specific value frequently commented upon by foreign observers. This observation is borne out by the popularity of the heroes manufactured in Hollywood and in the world of sports, by the advertisements of styles and cosmetics. As the average age of the population increases, this value is already showing signs of being given new interpretations in terms of geriatrics, etc. This will be alluded to again in following paragraphs.

2. *Material Well-Being*

If indeed effort is optimistically viewed in a material universe that man can master, then material well-being is a consistent concomitant value. Not only is it consistent within the value system, but it has been amply demonstrated in our national experience. It has been manifest in the American standard of living. The nation's geographic frontier and its natural resources, combined with an era of invention, have convinced most Americans of the validity of such a proposition. In the American scene progress and prosperity have come to have almost identical meaning. So deeply convinced are most Americans of what is generally called "prosperity" that material well-being is close to being considered a "right" due to those who have conscientiously practiced the specific value of work. The congruence of this view with the new science of geriatrics, social insurance, and the growth of investment trusts is obvious. It represents a consistent adjustment of specific values to a changing situation. However, as the situational context changes it may weaken the present linkage between effort and optimism with the resulting devaluation of both and thereby set up a new strain for consistency that may alter the present configuration of the American value system.

One of the most common stereotypes about the United States is its materialism. Viewed in the context of the value system presented here, materialism is less a value *per se* than an optimistic assertion of two value premises (mastery over material nature and the perfectibility of man) that have operated in a favorable environment. What foreign observers may call materialism, with derogatory or envious innuendos, is to the American a success that carries the moral connotation of "rightness"—of a system that proves itself or, as Americans would say with complete consistency, that "works." Within the frame of American value premises, success phrased as material well-being resolves the material-spiritual opposition and becomes a proof of right-mindedness. "Hard work pays off." The old and widely known proverb that, "Virtue is its own reward" has a particularly American slant, meaning not that virtue is in itself a reward but rather that virtue is rewarded.

If hard work is a "good thing" in a material universe and since it has been rewarded by material well-being, consistency requires that manual labor should be accorded dignity or, at least, should not be considered undignified. Furthermore, manual labor is an unambiguous manifestation of that activism alluded to earlier.

The salience of material well-being as a focal value in American life leads into many byways, some of which confuse and confound members of societies founded on a different value configuration. In military terms, for example, Americans are so profoundly convinced of the correctness of the material well-being formula that logistics forms our basic strategy. Personal heroism, though it may amply exist, is not assumed to be the fundamental requisite for victory, as it is in France. In American terms, victory is won by the sheet of matériel laid down in front of advancing infantry and by the lines of supply that must be built up to provide such a barrier [against] hand-to-hand combat.

In the same vein, there is little room in the American middle-class value system for the realities of physical pain, brutality, and death. Since they are nonetheless natural and undeniable, they are given a highly stylized treatment in detective fiction, newspapers, and movies that provide an acceptable discharge of tension created by the discrepancy between values and reality. Many Americans are alienated and morally repelled when they encounter the poverty and misery prevalent in certain lands. They manage to go through life untouched experientially even by those in our own

population who have not succeeded—those who exist hopelessly
in rural or urban slums or those who are victims of physical or
psychic disasters. We have provided for the latter so effectively
that they are whisked away into institutions that our national
surpluses permit us to provide comparatively lavishly. Death itself
has been surrounded with appurtenances of asepsis. Evelyn
Waugh's *The Loved One* could never have been written with
India as a setting. The compelling quality of this value emerges
when we consider world statistics on human welfare facilities. In
this respect, the United States is consistently in the lead. Yet, if
we compare these statistics with the outbursts of compassion that
a newspaper account of a "blue baby" will elicit, we become
aware not only of the power of this focal value but also the re-
sultant constellation that might be summarized as compulsive com-
passionate activism.

3. *Conformity*

Viewed historically it seems probable that conformity is a more
recent focal value in American culture than effort-optimism and
material well-being. It may represent one of the valuational changes
induced by the strain for consistency assumed in the paper to be
one of the forces that alter value systems. Over a century ago De
Tocqueville saw with singular clarity the potential threat to national solidarity inherent in the values of individual liberty, on the
one hand, and of the sovereignty of enfranchised masses, on the
other hand. In the contemporary American value system, conformity represents an attempt to resolve this dilemma. The France of
today, with a comparable dilemma, has still to find a resolution.

If the premises of perfectibility and equality are linked with the
focal value labeled effort-optimism, then each middle-class American may legitimately aspire to maximal self-realization. But, if
man is to master through his efforts a mechanistic universe, he
must cooperate with his fellow men, since no single man can master
the universal machine. In other words, people are individuated
and prized, but if they are to cooperate with their fellow men for
mastery of the universe or, in more modest terms, of the immediate
physical and sociopolitical environment, too great a degree of individualization would be an impediment. Also since the American

value premises—in contradistinction to much of the rest of the world—include equality, the realization of the self in such a context would not necessarily imply the development of highly personalized and idiosyncratic but rather of egalitarian traits. Self-cultivation in America has as its goal less the achievement of uniqueness and more the achievement of similarity. This is a proposition many Frenchmen, for example, find difficult to grasp. The Japanese, with their stress upon self-cultivation in order more perfectly to discharge the obligations they owe their family and society, might come closer to understanding this American formulation.[4]

The assimilation of diverse immigrant groups to middle-class American values has been one of the remarkable sociopolitical achievements of the nation and testifies to the compelling vigor of its value system. As resources and space were more fully manned, the very lack of tolerance for differences that facilitated assimilation was finally to curtail the admission to this country of those who presented such differences.

Earlier in our history self-reliance and initiative were specific values attached to the focal value of liberty. Today these specific values have a new focus. Individual self-reliance and initiative are attached to the promotion of the commonweal and to the progress of society. Conformity has replaced liberty as a focal value to which these specific traits are attached. Cooperation has been added as a specific value that has facilitated the shift-over. The present American value system manifests a highly effective integration of the individual to society.

The ramification of this nexus into the sphere of education has been alluded to already. Education is envisaged as a means by which all men through effort can realize themselves. But since cooperativeness is a specific value also inserted into this equation, education comes to be envisaged as a means to make more men more effective workers and better citizens. The land-grant colleges, the vast network of public schools, and the system of free and compulsory education with its stress on education for citizenship

---

[4] For a formulation of Japanese values see William Caudill, "Japanese-American Personality and Acculturation," *Genetic Psychology Monographs* 45 (1952) pp. 3-102. On page 93 the author points out the compatibility of Japanese and American middle-class values.

and on technical skills have set the American educational system apart from that of many other countries. In the American context the linkage between conformity, effort-optimism, and material well-being leads inevitably to mass education with the emphasis on the common man rather than the uncommon man, to its technical and practical cast, to what seems to many observers its low standards. Simultaneously, to many Americans schooling has acquired the weight of a goal rather than a means. A college degree is a "good thing" in itself, whether or not the education entailed is prized. This concatenation does not lead one to expect perfection as a directive for performance in American life.

In a society where cooperation and good citizenship are valued and where the commonweal is served by having each man develop himself through his own efforts, a generous friendliness, openness, and relaxation of interpersonal relations are not only possible but desirable so long as the associated expanding economy furnishes the situational possibilities. Rigid class structures and protective privacies are inconsistent with the values here enumerated. Doors need not be closed to rooms; fences need not be built around properties. The tall hedges of England and the enclosing walls of France are not appropriate to the American scene, where life faces outward rather than inward. If every individual is as "good as" the next and all are good citizens—what is there to hide? The open front yards, the porches, or more recently the picture windows that leave the home open to everyone's view, the figurative and literal klieg lights under which our public figures live are all evidence of the value placed in American life on likeness and the pressure exerted for conformity. This is very different from saying that American middle-class individuals are in fact all alike. It means merely that likeness is valued.

The American hostility to figures in authority has been frequently noted, and in this connection the almost placatory informality and familiarity of American manners that serve to play down status differences have been pointed out. The apparent contradiction between the striving for upward mobility and the distrust of those who achieve pre-eminent positions can now be seen in more balanced terms. If the argument advanced here is correct, upward mobility is valued as successful activity, but when it reaches a point where it outstrips the premise of equality and the local value of conformity it borders on *hubris*.

In this connection then the relaxed, friendly manner of American life so frequently commented upon by foreign observers can be gauged in the broader context of an adjustment to incompatible values. The search for popularity, the desire to be liked, the wish to be considered a "good fellow," are searches for reassurance that, in striving to achieve all the ends implied by the focal value of effort-optimism, one has not exceeded the bounds set by the other focal value of conformity. That this process can operate at any level of actual achievement, from the presidency of the United States to chairmanship of an Elks Club committee, need not be stressed. It is the boss, the politician, the teacher, the "big shots" who are disvalued figures to the extent that their superordinate position implies authority. It is the movie star and the baseball hero who are valued figures since their pre-eminence connotes no authority but at the same time dramatizes the meteoric rise to fame and popularity through hard work and youthful striving.

Another aspect of American social life is thrown into relief in the effort to balance effort-optimism, material well-being, and conformity and their linked specific values. In the business and financial world, despite conservative tendencies, there has been a steady trend toward consolidation and standardization. Although the familiar and now perhaps inappropriate hue and cry is still raised about monopoly and big business, the latter, at least, serves the greater material well-being of the American mass consumer, whose values are geared to conformity. "Big business" is consonant with the American value system here portrayed so long as the owners of such enterprises are pictured as the American middle class, so long as savings are invested in the stocks and bonds of these enterprises so that the middle class shares "equally" in its successes, and so long as the authorities in such enterprises are presented as servants of the people. In these terms the American value system is served. The dangers of a too extreme individualistic power-centered authority are thus allayed, and competitive rivalry is brought under control.

Summary and Conclusions

Two basic assumptions were made: (1) that no viable value

system *qua* system can entertain logical contraries, and (2) that there is a strain for consistency among the spurious contradictions that may be inherent in any value system. Four major premises were assumed to underlie the American middle-class value system: (1) a mechanistically conceived universe, (2) man's mastery over that universe, (3) the equality of men, and (4) man's perfectibility. From these four premises three focal values were suggested: (1) effort-optimism, (2) material well-being, and (3) conformity. Each of these focal values is envisaged as being more or less directly derived from each of the premises. Each in turn constitutes a series (here not fully explored) of specific values and directives. Each of the three focal values and their constituent specific values are more or less consistently interlocked. But the viability of a value system does not rest exclusively on its internal coherence. It must also manifest a considerable degree of congruence with the situational context within which it exists. Changes in value systems will result, therefore, from a strain for consistency not only within the value system but also between values and situational factors.

C. Commentary and Analysis

The mutual reinforcement that occurs between the *basic premises* and their *focal values* in the light of the major *directions of change* should be underlined. This mutual strengthening within the American cultural value profile shows a system with deep inner consistency, a consistency which may well account for the vigor and widespread adoption throughout the world of the "American way of life."

Within the system of directions, premises and focal values we can hope to situate ourselves and find a meaning for work. For the system helps us to understand and explain the "why" of many of our present-day behavior patterns. Just as we can use these insights of the anthropologist to trace the cultural pathways by which we as a nation of people travelled from the Puritans of Plymouth Rock to the launching pad at Cape Kennedy, we can also show how much of our current behavior represents a continuous and consistent adjustment of specific values to a changing situation, and in some way foresee what is to come.

The fecundity of the anthropological insights is clear when we interpret the directives and focal values in terms of a common psychosocial conflict between the value of the individual person and the value of the community. Our society, in general, seems to be striving to make us a nation of *securely standardized individual personalities*. Security is proposed as the fruit of *material well-being;* the desire for "more" and "quicker" material products introduces the value of *conformity,* which means standardization, anonymity and the sovereignty of the collectivity; on the other hand, the desire for "bigger" and "better" material products encourages the *effort-optimism* value, which induces individualization, self-realization, status-seeking.

The opposition between the movements toward a standardization of personality through conformity and toward the development of the uniquely individual personality through effort-optimism produces the conflict we are discussing.

This conflict between conformity and individuality has been faced by our culture by the employment of three adaptive techniques: (1) mobility, (2) service, and (3) consolidation-cooperation. Examples of mobility are seen in our American premium on friendliness, openness and social popularity. As examples of human service and of having life "face outward" we see the burgeoning peace and anti-poverty corps, lists of philanthropic foundations and the general trend to have figures of authority assume the attitude of public "servants." Consolidation-cooperation techniques show themselves in team research, team teaching, the formation of unions and economic cooperatives.

The three techniques which our culture has been utilizing to help solve the personality conflicts posed by the opposition between the focal values of conformity and effort-optimism are tending to create another focal value in our culture: *the value of the person and interpersonal relationship.* The importance of the person and interpersonal relationships has long been recognized and fostered by the existentialist and personalist philosophers and was acknowledged later by the psychological and psychoanalytic disciplines. They are now being inserted as a formal value into the cultural behavior of the American people. And the conflict between conformity and individuality takes on an added depth with the new focal value.

This development in our culture leads us to consider in the work context the mutual influence of the organization and the individual personality. On the one hand, the individual sometimes helps and sometimes hinders the growth and effectiveness of an organization; on the other hand, the organization sometimes nourishes but often curtails personality development. The problem of personality in the midst of bureaucracy, the burden of the following chapter, is viewed from the eyes of the social psychologist and the economist.

In this commentary we are placing less stress upon the theological dimensions of our reflection, finding it more profitable to tie together a number of points made in the selection from Du Bois' writings and to reflect upon the basic point the anthropologist is trying to make and which so many people miss. For example, many of the Christian catechists writing and teaching today, who intend to base their thought and practice on the findings of the social sciences, forget a fundamental insight of the anthropologist: that the intellectual and conceptual communication to a person of an attitude does not necessarily result in a corresponding modification of his customary behavior. Human beings have an uncanny ability for *believing* one thing and *behaving* in a contradictory way.

Behavioral customs usually become habitual only over a long period which includes many repetitions of the behavioral activity. In forming a habit, many imaginative, attitudinal and sensory associations combine in the repetition of a pattern of responses to a situation. Through such repetitions habits are formed, which become customary behavior. When such habits are ingrained in the organism and personality, it is difficult to eradicate them and replace them with new behavior. Seldom does a simple change of attitude or a new intellectual conviction result in a deep-seated behavioral change. It takes a long time to replace a well-integrated habit with a new one, especially when the new habit has small integration-potential within the present attitudinal and behavioral setting of the individual and community. Thus, not only must the catechist be very patient when trying to inculcate a new attitude in his subject, but he must recognize that unless he can fit the new conviction into the attitudinal and behavioral setting he finds there, the catechist should hope for no long-lasting success.

On the other hand, whenever we can convey new ideas in terms of other well-known ideas, and whenever there exist attitudes or values to which such new ideas can be connected, and finally if the behavioral implications of the new ideas can be induced in terms of behavioral patterns already customary, then we have the best chance of producing an effective and lasting change both in attitude and behavior. For example, once black-and-white television and the watching habits of the nation are well integrated into the everyday life of individuals, it is relatively easy to introduce color television. It is acceptable, in that it fits the behavior and attitudes of our society. Many easily-avoidable mistakes have been made in the introduction of the new liturgy into the life of American Catholicism. The point here is to understand this fundamental principle of the cultural anthropologist and not to forget it when reflecting upon a practical and concrete Christian meaning of the world of work and in forming the Christian's attitudes and behavior in this world of work.

Constructing such behavioral and value profiles as were presented in this chapter is the task of the cultural anthropologist. The studies of cultures and national character are available for most countries of the world. A presentation of the cultural directives and focal values such as Cora Du Bois has given us for the United States are invaluable tools not only for the catechist but for all Christians who wish to give Christ to the world. Through a knowledge of values, attitudes, motives and their corresponding behavioral patterns the Christian possesses a powerful means of communicating with the world about him.

It is important to realize that an awareness of such values, attitudes and motives would also help the Christian to better understand and direct his own life and ways of acting. This is another manifestation of the tendency, which we saw in the chapter on the worker and his education, toward the integration of all human activity, personal and productive, in an individual's life and within the community.

Questions for Discussion

1. What is a culture? Is it a product of heredity?
2. What are the roots of the dominant value system of middle-class Americans? What are the two basic assumptions of the study? What four major premises regarding man in his relation to the universe underlie this value system?
3. What three focal values in American society does Cora Du Bois isolate?
4. Describe the way in which each of them affects the approach to work.
5. Of what use are anthropological insights for a Christian understanding of work? Discuss.

VII
THE WORKER
AND THE ORGANIZATION

A. Prenote

In this chapter we look at work through the eyes of the organization and see how the corporation views the individual worker. Among the primary goals of the corporation or institution in American society, such as General Motors or Montgomery Ward, are economic growth and development. Thanks to the sociologist and social psychologist involved in industry, we recognize and realize that the employee in his daily occupation seeks many more rewards than salary, and that efficiency in operation and achievement of production goals of an industrial organization are dependent upon more motivational factors than the largeness of the employee's paycheck.

In an article written especially for this book from the viewpoint of the social psychologist, A. G. Brown, S.J. surveys and evaluates three approaches (scientific management, human relations, and structuralist) which organizations utilize in attempting to create and maintain a work setting in which, at least in theory, workers may profit the corporation by continually improving in productive efficiency, and at the same time find social, emotional and financial satisfaction in their tasks.

B. Selection: The Individual and the Group at Work in Contemporary Society

The Social Environment of Modern Work

To say that contemporary man spends most of his working life

within the context of a society characterized by the presence of
large-scale bureaucratic organizations is a fact that few students
of modern society would deny. In fact, no aspect of modern social
life is unaffected by the organizational trend: work, play, education, politics, religion.[1] And insofar as work is concerned, contemporary conditions affect all classes or categories of men at work:
executives, white collar workers, craftsmen, assembly line workers,
and manual laborers. Present-day reflection on the problem of
the relationship between the individual and the group is incomplete if this fact is not reckoned with. The purpose of this essay
is to consider this relationship within the context of the modern
work situation. At issue is the question of how the individual in
his unique individuality is best for the modern work group situation, and how, in turn, this group situation may best enhance the
personality of the individual worker. The dimensions of the question are manifold and complex, and they are by no means settled.
However, it is hoped that the remarks to follow will serve to ac-
quaint the reader with the basic nature of the problem.

The bureaucratic structure of the large-scale work organization
provides for a social environment within which two types of social
groups develop, the *formal group,* which is of the essence of
bureaucratic organization, and the *informal group,* a type of human social association which arises spontaneously within and frequently in spite of the formal group structure. Formal groups are
created by the organization in order to insure that individual action
is rationally related to efficient realization of the goals or purposes
of the organization.[2] In such a structure there is an integrated
series of hierarchized work positions to which adhere a number
of obligations and privileges strictly defined by specific regulations.
Each of these positions contains elements of delegated responsibility and authority which inhere in the position itself, and not in the
particular individual who happens to occupy a given position at
a given time. The formal group structure which results from this

---

[1] Amitai Etzioni, *Modern Organizations* (Englewood Cliffs, N.J.: Prentice-
Hall, 1964), p. 1.
[2] Robert K. Merton, *Social Theory and Social Structure* (Glencoe, Ill.:
Free Press, 1957), pp. 195-96.

type of rational planning tends to stress the depersonalization of social relationships. It is perhaps natural therefore that informal social association develops within the formal structure.

Individuals in modern organizations are formally called upon to perform only certain strictly regulated activities in order to fulfill their organizational role. However, it is the whole man who works for the organization and because he has needs beyond the minimum ones of doing his allotted task, he seeks fulfillment of some of these needs by spontaneously developing a variety of informal social relationships with other members of the organization. Thus arises the informal group.[3] A social group, in the most generic sense, consists of a number of individuals who psychologically perceive that they have certain common interests, and who interact with one another on the basis of these shared common interests. The formal group structure of the large-scale organization provides for the physical proximity required for individuals to become mutually aware of common interests. Unlike the depersonalization present in formal structure, the social relationships which flourish within the informal group setting are highly personal and meaningful to the individuals involved. They provide the context for the satisfaction of those needs which go beyond the specific job, and they are the basis for the development of friendship cliques within the organization. Moreover, it is possible for the informal group to define standards of work and production, quite independently and at times at odds with the standards set forth by the rational planning involved in the establishment of the formal structure of the organization. A conflict of this nature is most likely to occur when there is present a high level of individual or group dissatisfaction with the formal structure. Such a conflict is actually part of the broader and more inclusive organizational dilemma involving the rationality of formal group structure on the one hand, and individual well-being on the other.

Two Approaches to the Organizational Dilemma

What is the best approach to follow in order to insure that the

---

[3] Edgar H. Schein, *Organizational Psychology* (Englewood Cliffs, N.J.: Prentice-Hall, 1965), pp. 67-69.

individual in his individuality is best for the work group, and to guarantee in turn that the work group situation enhances the personality of the individual worker? The approach that is followed in a specific organization will depend in large degree on the particular theory of motivation which is adhered to there. Two approaches which have been applied to the modern work situation are the approach of *scientific management* and the *human relations* approach. They are unalike primarily because of the differing theories of human motivation upon which they are based.[4]

The scientific management approach arose as a response to a search for greater effectiveness and efficiency in large-scale organizations, and it was initiated by Frederick W. Taylor in his book on *Scientific Management* (New York: Harper, 1911). According to this slightly scientific approach, the individual worker is considered to be motivated to work solely by fear of hunger and by the related drive for maximum economic profit. He is viewed as an economic man, and if material rewards are closely related to work efforts, the worker will respond with the maximum performance he is capable of. Payment, therefore, is made to the worker on the basis of performance alone, and no other criteria are applied. Time and motion studies determine and define the physical capabilities of the individual worker, and the formal group structure of the organization is then structured in such a way as to relate these pre-determined capabilities of the worker to the means of production in the most rational and efficient manner possible. It is obvious that the approach of scientific management to the problem of the relationship of the individual to the work group stresses the importance of the formal and highly organized group. Thus the individual worker must fit into a pre-determined structure which is characterized by a clearly defined division of labor which is, in turn, highly specialized. The lines of authority and responsiblility are rigid and not subject to modification by individual action. Informal associations of workers which spontaneously arise within the context of the work situation are virtually ignored.

In striking contrast to scientific management, and largely in reaction to it, the human relations approach recognizes and empha-

---

4 Etzioni, pp. 20-41.

sizes the importance of the informal group in the modern work situation. Elton Mayo, regarded as the founder of the human relations approach, recognized that non-economic factors play an important role in the motivation of the individual worker. His insights led to a series of studies conducted at the Western Electric Company's Hawthorne Works in Chicago from 1927 to 1932, which are reported in *Management and the Worker,* by F. J. Roethlisberger and W. J. Dickson (Cambridge: Harvard, 1939). The Hawthorne studies indicated that emotional, unplanned, non-rational elements are important factors in organizational behavior. Individual workers bring a variety of social and cultural needs to the work situation, and the satisfaction of these needs, or the lack thereof, figures significantly in levels of production and efficiency attained by the formal work group. Thus the establishment of amicable social relationships with co-workers and the establishment of mutual respect among workers are factors which enter into the motivation of the individual worker. The informal social groups which develop in response to these needs define and determine norms of production which are generally more representative of the true levels of output than are the pre-determined norms established by the formal structure of the organization. In sum, individual work behavior is anchored in the informal group. Overall organizational efficiency is enhanced when full advantage is taken of the social relationships which develop within this context. Such factors as leadership, emotional communication, and meaningful participation are not considered in the formal group structure with its emphasis on specialization, efficiency, and strictly defined levels of authority and responsibility. However, the integration of the individual with the group in the work situation cannot be accomplished by ignoring the formal structure of the organization. This is the built-in weakness of the human relations approach and it is due to the tendency of this approach to take a pejorative view of formal structure.

The two approaches to the organizational dilemma thus far discussed are in many ways diametrically opposed to one another. The factors one approach sees as critical and crucial, the other hardly considers, and the variables one views as central, the other largely ignores. However, the two approaches have one element

in common: neither sees any basic contradiction or insoluble dilemma in the relationship between the rationality of formal group
structure and the well-being of the individual worker. On the one
hand, scientific management, an approach which in its pure form
does not enjoy too much currency today, assumes that the most
efficient organization is also the most satisfying one, since it will
maximize both productivity and the economic return to the economically motivated individual worker. The formal group structure
is the best context within which to attain this double goal. On the
other hand, human relations, an approach which is still widely
accepted in organizational circles, assumes that the most satisfying
organization is also the most efficient one, since it maximizes satisfaction of all the individual's needs and thereby enhances the efficiency of individual and group participation in the work situation.
The familial environment encouraged by the informal group is perceived to be the ideal context in which to achieve the double goal.

The Structuralist Approach

Efforts to construct a synthesis from the valid insights of the
formal or scientific management approach and the informal or
human relations approach characterizes the current trend in organizational theory. This synthesis, known as the structuralist approach, provides a more realistic context within which to discuss
the problem of the relationship between the individual and the
work group.[5] It is not simply a matter of which type of work
group, formal or informal, provides the social environment within
which the individual in his individuality is best for the group, and
within which the work group enhances the well-being of the individual worker. The context for the structuralists is the over-all
organizational structure, composed of both formal and informal
elements. It should also be noted that whereas the two earlier
approaches focused almost exclusively on industrial and business
organizations, the structuralist approach makes possible a broader
view of the modern work situation by extending research to prisons,
hospitals, churches, schools, and armies. This broader base of research indicates a recognition of the fact that practically all types

---

[5] Etzioni, pp. 41-49.

of modern work are performed within the context of large-scale organizations.

Unlike the limited theories of human motivation which constitute the starting points for the approaches of scientific management and human relations, the theory which forms the basis for an attempt to indicate how the over-all organization enhances the relationship between the individual and the group should encompass the totality of human needs that serve as motivating forces in the life of the individual at work. A. H. Maslow proposes such a comprehensive theory, and it is possible to relate it to the structuralist synthesis.[6] Maslow notes that the motivation of the individual at work may be viewed in terms of a hierarchy of human needs which requires a satisfactory level of fulfillment if the individual is to achieve a sense of well-being in the work situation. Ranging from the lowest to the highest point in the hierarchy, the five general types of needs include the *physiological, safety, belonging, status,* and the need for *self-actualization.*

The two types of needs on the lowest levels of the hierarchy constitute needs that are most directly related to the physical integrity of the person. On one hand, individuals engage in work in order to acquire the economic resources necessary to provide for the *physiological necessities* of the body. Moreover, when the worker is the head of a family, as is usually the case, he is responsible for the physical well-being of the members of his family. Resources must be available for the provision of adequate food, shelter, and medical care. These needs motivate the individual to secure a level of economic remuneration for work performed which will enable him to meet these basic needs of human existence. On the other hand, *safety needs* involve the avoidance of work situations which may prove harmful to the physical health of the individual. And since the conditions of work needed to ensure a high level of safety are generally controlled by the organization, the individual is motivated to secure work with an organization which offers a reasonable guarantee of providing for his physical

---

[6] Maslow's theory of human motivation is summarized in the book by H. C. Smith, *Psychology of Industrial Behavior* (New York: McGraw-Hill, 1964), pp. 24-36.

well-being. It is true that certain individuals are motivated by high economic return to work under hazardous conditions. This fact, however, does not negate the relevancy of safety needs as a factor in worker motivation, as indicated by the currency of this issue in negotiations between labor and management in modern industry.

The third and fourth levels in the hierarchy of human needs proposed by Maslow deal with the social needs of the individual for belonging and status. *Belonging needs* refer to the individual's need for acceptance by others, a feeling achieved largely through the establishment of meaningful social relationships. The individual realizes this, either consciously or unconsciously, when he enters the work situation, and he is motivated by it because of his long experience of dependency on parents and peers while growing to adulthood. This reservoir of experience makes the individual aware of the fact that many of his needs are fulfilled only through association with others. Within the work situation, the worker feels a strong need to be accepted and liked by his work group and to a greater or less degree, depending on the particular individual involved, he fears the work group's rejection of him. Thus the individual is motivated to work for that organization which has a social environment that offers him a reasonable opportunity to achieve a meaningful sense of belonging.

The individual's *need for status* within the work situation is related to the fact that all persons in a social group occupy particular positions in the group, all of which have specific privileges and obligations attached to them. An individual's status within the group is defined by his position in that group. In work group situations, some workers have positions that are recognized as being more important, or of higher status, than the positions of other workers within the group. The need to maintain and increase the importance of one's social position is a factor that enters into the motivation of the individual worker.

On the highest level of the hierarchy is the human *need for self-actualization,* a need which motivates the individual to seek the realization of his potential and to become what he is capable of becoming. Unlike the other four needs in the hierarchy, which are satisfied by the presence in the environment of conditions external to the individual, the need for self-actualization pertains to the inner man. In the work situation this need is related to engaging in work that is at once productive and self-satisfying, thereby allowing the individual to work in accord with his talents and abilities.

It is necessary now to consider how the social environment of modern work contributes to the satisfaction of the human needs outlined above. However, before proceeding it should be noted that the environment of work is not the only environment which caters to these needs, especially those of belonging, status, and self-actualization. On the contrary, the experiences of the individual in the family and the community are of equal importance.[7] The effort of the human relations approach to emphasize the informal group and to promote a familial spirit at work tends to overlook the significance of the extra-work environment in which the individual lives. Work is one of the activities of man, not the sole activity. However, the two environments are related. Financial reward and status at work affect belonging and status in the extra-work environment. At the other extreme, emphasis on the formal group in the approach of scientific management tends to involve a virtual denial of the relevancy of the work group environment for the realization of the other than purely economic needs of the individual. Work may not be the sole activity of man, but it is one of the more significant activities that all men engage in. Consequently, the social environment of work is of some importance to the well-being of man. In turn, the well-being of man at work is of significance to the resolution of the organizational dilemma posed by the social environment of modern work.

The role of the formal and informal aspects of over-all organizational structure in satisfying human needs is affected by the tendency of higher needs in the hierarchy to take on more significance insofar as lower needs are fulfilled. Informal structure is especially relevant to the higher needs of belonging, status, and self-actualization, whereas formal structure caters to all five types of general needs. In this regard, the formal structure which is created by the organization in order to insure that individual action is rationally related to efficient realization of organizational

---

[7] Leonard R. Sayles, *Individualism and Big Business* (New York: McGraw-Hill, 1963), p. 75.

goals affects the well-being of the individual worker. His physiological needs for food, shelter, and medical care are satisfied insofar as rational structure promotes high profit levels to the organization and satisfying financial rewards to the worker. In addition, the specific work regulations prescribed by the formal structure enhance the possibilities of working within a safe environment. This is not the case when safety regulations are left to develop by chance.

Organizational efficiency and the human needs for belonging and status are best realized in an environment in which the obligations and privileges of each position within the work group are clearly defined. In such an environment individuals know what the conditions are for fulfilling these needs and they can order their behavior accordingly. The structure of the formal work group provides this clarity. The informal group structure also contributes to these social needs. The individual need for belonging is fulfilled by the personal social relationships which develop within the context of the informal associations which emerge at work. The sense of belonging thereby attained contributes in turn to over-all organizational efficiency. Insofar as status needs are concerned, the leadership which generally develops in the informal group is an important source of satisfaction for the individual. The organization benefits when areas of responsibility and authority specified in the formal structure are related to lines of informal group leadership.

Finally, the possibility of fulfilling the need for self-actualization is increased when the individual knows just how he can best use his talents and develop his potential. The job descriptions for each work position provided by the organizational structure outline the specifications for each position within the formal work group. Knowing these, the individual is able to judge both where he best fits, and what type of specialized training to pursue in order to improve his chances to realize his potential. By providing for human needs in this way, the formal work group structure guarantees, on the one hand, that the individual in his individuality is best for the work group situation, and, on the other hand, that the situation is best for the personal development and well-being of the individual worker. In addition, a worker is most satisfied, and the organization benefits most, when the responsibilities of the job are such as to encourage the individual to use all his skill and ingenuity. Due to its rigidity, the formal structure may inhibit this process. However, the sense of well-being and acceptance which develops within the informal group can provide an environment which will encourage the individual to exercise his ingenuity, even when such ingenuity may lead to modifications of the work process not explicitly provided for by the formal structure.

In sum, it is possible for both the formal and informal aspects of organizational structure to contribute to the attainment of organizational goals and to the well-being of the worker. In this regard, however, two points should be kept in mind, namely, a working integration between the formal and informal aspects of organizational structure must be achieved, and at the same time, a state of complete harmony is not necessary or even desirable. The vital factor in achieving a realistic degree of integration between the formal and informal revolves about the problem of achieving goals which are shared by the individual and the organization. The more goals in common an organization and its workers can develop, and the better their different goals can be fitted together, the more fully realized will be the potentialities of the organization and its members. Some significant questions related to this problem are as follows: How do the informal groups in the organization relate to the formal structure of the work group? Are the two types of groups working at cross purposes? Are all or most or only a few of the individuals in any one formal work group also members of one informal group? Do informal groups cut across formal divisions, or do they tend to parallel them? Does informal group leadership conflict with the leadership provided for by the formal organizational structure? The answers to questions such as the above provide the basis for estimating the degree of integration present.

At the same time, a state of total harmony is not necessary or even desirable. Conflict is viewed as undesirable by the approach of scientific management, and even more so by the human relations approach, which seeks to maximize organizational harmony. The structuralists, however, point to the many important and varied social functions of conflict, including the positive contribution it can make to over-all organizational efficiency. The expression of conflict, within limits, allows genuine differences of interests to emerge, whose resolution may lead to an adjustment of the organizational system to the real situation and hence to greater efficiency in operation and to a more satisfying work environment for individuals. If ignored or artificially smothered, conflict and its concomitant latent alienation will lead to impaired efficiency. Recall that the informal group is a type of human social association which arises spontaneously within and possibly in spite of the formal group structure. The two types of groups will work at cross purposes if there is no recognition on the formal level of the interests that exist on the informal level.

The structuralist approach to the organizational dilemma discussed above represents an attempt to secure the well-being of both the organization and the individual. Both goals are possible of attainment provided that the place of the individual within the total social environment of modern work is taken into consideration. Moreover, the structuralist approach is unlike the approaches of scientific management and human relations in that it does not seek to achieve a complete resolution of the dilemma. Rather, it seeks a realistic, working integration between the formal and informal aspects of organizational structure, an integration which will in turn promote the common interests and recognize the conflicting interests of the organization and the individual.

C. Commentary and Analysis

The point of emphasis of our reflection in this chapter is *community*. For the Christian, more than ever before in the history of the Church, this is an age of community. It is perhaps the first time since the early Church that Christians are being forced to discover or rediscover the sense of community, for it is only through the solidarity and sharing which belongs to a community that certain problems which today face us can be solved.

No one can deny that essentially there is a solidarity among mankind, if only a biological one. Furthermore, through Adam we are all one in sin, and through Christ we are all invited to be one in grace. Nevertheless, when we are faced with the daily problems of cooperating with one another in communal enterprises in the family and work situations, for example, such theological principles of unity in sin and grace offer the concrete situation little more than the assurance that radically we are one.

In the practical sphere the "world" has taught us many lessons. When the labor force in this country was faced with the choice of unity or extinction at the beginning of the century, workers developed means of uniting quite successfully. When the community of scientists and inventors was given tasks to do and equipment to construct, such as the cyclotron or the technological complex we call Cape Kennedy — tasks which could not even be conceived by one man's mind — the scientists learned how to consolidate and coordinate techniques and how to sit down together and communicate.

The development of community (in a variety of senses of the word) goes on daily in the research and production branches of corporations, large and small. Brown's article presents three social psychological techniques which organizations today employ to establish productively efficient communities among their employees.

At this point, the Christian makes two observations. The first is that the phenomenon of a growing sense of community and the recognition of the importance of cooperation and solidarity among men are not the special possession of the Christian community. We have much to learn from the world of business in this regard. In this situation, however, it is consoling to notice that the phenomenon of community is developing in a parallel manner in both the Church and the world. The goals of communion among persons, communion in goods and communion in action, are much the same in both structures.

The second observation is that the corporations have spent much more time, money and effort in attempting to solve the practical problems of formal and informal groups than the Christian community has. Since the fundamental goals of cooperation and "productivity" of the corporation are similar to those of the Church, there is no reason why the Christian community cannot profit from the discoveries of the social sciences in this regard and apply them to corresponding situations within the Christian community. There is much need for such understanding in the areas of worship and the religious life, as well as in the world of work.

Since the situations within the Christian community are not exactly the same as those in the productive organization, the objective of the Christian thinker would be not merely to borrow techniques and apply them to specific problem areas in the Christian community. This would only reach part of the larger quest, which is to achieve the Christian community.

Most theologians would agree that today we are in the "age of the resurrection," hence an age of community. For hope and confidence and optimism, which are strongly in evidence today, are much more community virtues than suffering, passion and sin. However, without denying that we are one in sin and that the sin of one man affects the entire community, we can *emphasize* optimism and hope and the fact that the kindness and love of one man affects the entire community also, even more effectively than sin in many cases.

We also know that God in Christ created the material world for us. As long as we look upon this gift with uneasiness, because it has the capacity to offer us the material occasion for sin, we can never enter with total openness into the world of work. And until we can learn to greet the world with this eagerness we will never discover what wisdom and mystery the earth and our brothers have to offer us and share with us.

If however we come to see the world as the vehicle for our solidarity (insofar as it can be) with one another and with Christ, then we enter the world of the corporation and big business with open eyes. We enter there, not to borrow but to learn, not to glance at things and run away, but to accept the invitation to enter in, to discover how and why the persons there communicate and cooperate. The groups within the organization do not enjoy the unity of the blessed in heaven, but they do work together, some with more interest and enthusiasm than others. Here with Christian insight we must discover what is effective in promoting unity and what is not.

If God wishes us Christians to grow in the sense of community in our personal and productive lives, then we should study and experience as Christians the personal and productive communities which fill the streets and highways of our country. To form the most personal and productive Christian community we shall have to build upon the human structures and techniques which surround us. Two observations from the principles of the social psychologist are important to note.

First of all, it is a fact, perhaps unfortunate, that we Christians have a long-standing tradition of individualistic piety, which has had its bad effect in previous attempts at community enterprises. On the other hand, in the organization, the social psychologist is concerned with the individual worker as individual, but he is much more concerned with the individual as he works *with* others and, more especially, *for* others. In this regard there is much that the Christian community can learn from the corporations concerning working with and for others.

Secondly, the employer realizes that his employee will be most productive and hence most profitable to his company if he can get the *whole man* to work for the organization. Thus, the employer realizes that a man's hands and muscles work more efficiently when his mind is interested in the work, when his imagination and creativity is stimulated, when the goals of his task are clear and inviting, when he enjoys feelings of success, progress and accomplishment, when he feels a sense of sociability and solidarity with those around him. And today we know that the secularized world of work employs the whole man. There are even times when a company goes overboard and tries to *own* the whole man, attempting to completely dictate to him how he should live his private life away from the organization. However, in general, mistakes such as these are soon corrected, for the organization finds that it is not profitable in the long run. It tends to destroy the spirit and creativity of the employee.

Practically, Christians can profit from the discoveries in group dynamics discovered by the industrial psychologist. There are many useless, annoying, and sometimes harmful effects of the structural system which forms the institutionalized side of the Church which could be eliminated with a modicum of effort, the insight to accomplish this task being already on hand courtesy of the research of the social scientists. Religious institutions could also profitably study the conclusions of the psychologists and sociologists in this regard.

We might also recall that motivation is generally heightened when the "worker" knows and understands the purposes and goals of the organization and is made to feel that he is a part of the corporation. Here the application to the Christian community at large as well as to subcommunities which go to make it up is obvious.

Questions for Discussion

1. What is the significance of the formal and informal group in large organizations?
2. What are some of the differences between the scientific management and the human relations approaches? What do these approaches have in common?
3. What advantages does the structuralist approach offer?
4. What are the five general types of human needs? How are they satisfied in the modern work environment? Explain.
5. What observations can a Christian make about the modern work community? What lessons can Christians learn from the work community?

VIII
WORK AND
ECONOMIC MAN

A. Prenote

Solutions to problems between bureaucracy and individual personality are difficult to achieve. Tensions exist and must be cared for in a healthy manner. Industrial psychology, industrial sociology, social psychology, organizational psychology, the science of decision making, studies in the human group: all these fields of interest are blossoming in universities and in industrial personnel research programs across the nation. Man is a social animal to a great degree in the work situation; the occupational context provides him with a "community" different from the other communities — social, political, familial — in which he also participates.

Man is, however, not only a social being but also an economic one. Similarly, no matter how much value an organization places upon social values whether among its own employees or within a large public context, the life blood of the organization is financial success; for, to survive at all a corporation must survive economically.

It is a commonplace today to hear a public speaker announce that our nation is entering a new socio-economic system. It is less common to find men who are willing to face the practical problems of social, psychological and economic security that are brought about by, for example, the fact of growing unemployment and the threat of abundance. Hardest of all, perhaps, is the search for men who are attempting to grapple seriously with the problems which will socio-economically face the nation in a decade or two. This lack of attention toward the future on a more general scale is understandable, for each corporation has enough problems of its own. The daily difficulties which arise in the economic sphere of an organization, such as coping with fraud, power strategy, ignorance, and bribery, sometimes develop into business situations where one may legitimately employ what are academically called the ethics of war. In such cases defensive tactics are the order of the day, and little true growth and progress is possible.

Nevertheless, socio-economic (as well as psychological and cultural) survival demands more than winning or losing ethical battles. National socio-economic survival and growth demand the recombination and reproportioning of the production factors of the economic function in the light of technology and the findings of the social sciences. Technology is perhaps the most important influence in the changing valence of each of the factors in the production function: capital, labor, management, land, natural resources. Historically, *power* in a society has generally been associated with one or other of the production factors. Only two centuries ago *capital* was recognized as a controller of power. Previous to this, *land* was the major influence on the direction of economic history. Today, however, it is to *technology* that corporations, organizations and nations turn for their source of economic, social and political power.

If our world is obsessed by technology and economic motivation, it is good to know that there are professional economists concerned about the human values in our automated nation. Technology seems to recognize no rule beyond itself; what technology can do it will do. Similarly, the deep-seated economic bent of our country exerts its own magnetic pull on the attitudes of men. In the light of the total allegiance demanded by both technology and profits, the factor of automation appears. Automation, which is gradually rendering human labor itself "redundant," catches us intellectually unprepared to deal with the effects of the economy and technology which automation has united and whose growth it continually fosters. It is this situation which Robert L. Heilbroner, an economist, attempts to assess. The selection was taken from the first issue of a new journal called *The Public Interest,* (1965), pp. 27-36. Heilbroner steps into the area of technology, where economists have always felt uncomfortable, and faces the economic implications of the automation question.

B. Selection: Men and Machines in Perspective

It is curious that technological unemployment has always been the intellectual stepchild of capitalism. One would think that nothing would have so interested economists as the economic impact — and above all, the impact on labor — of machines that suddenly alter the speed, the technical requirements, the human relationships, not to mention the end products, of the economic process. Instead, a consideration of technology in any guise has always made economists uncomfortable, and the thought of technology as a labor-affecting force has simply been too much for most of them. There was Marx, of course, who put technology and its labor-displacing effects into the very center of his diagnosis of capitalism, but no one paid any attention to him. Alfred Marshall and John Maynard Keynes, the two greatest economists of mature capitalism, managed to conduct their inquiries without admitting the subject of technology at all. Only in the underworld of economic thought, in the intellectual descendents of the Luddites, do we find a persisting concern with machines as things that do man's work and thereby lessen the need for his labor. But to the great majority of recognized economists these rude doubts remained as inadmissible as they were unexamined.

In itself, this is no doubt a subject for fruitful investigation—the problems society avoids are usually significant. But the long neglect of technology as a labor-displacing force also has an immediate relevance for our subject. It helps explain why automation catches us so intellectually unprepared. The necessary empirical data concerning technology, the essential statistical indicators of its impact on employment, simply do not exist, or are only now being hurriedly assembled. More important, in regard to the most elementary problems of theory—which is to say, in regard to the question of how to think about the question of technological unemployment—we find the same fuzzy notions, or the same dogmatic assertions masquerading as thought, that thirty-five years ago characterized our first attempts to explain the Great Depression.

So it is not surprising that the debate on automation is something less than a model of clarity. On the one hand we have the bland assurances of the Establishment that technological unemployment has never been more than a "frictional" problem for the economy; on the other hand, organizations with chilling names like "cyberculture" schedule the arrival of Total Unemployment for the day after tomorrow. In this fruitless exchange, two things are essentially missing. First, we lack some very important knowledge, the nature of which I will have a chance to point out as we go along. Second, we lack some kind of framework, compounded of history and theory, into which to put the current debate. It is the latter that I shall try to present in this article.

The Entrance of Technology

I wish to begin with a very simple proposition, although in our present state of unknowledge, it must be offered in a tentative rather than an assertive tone. It is that inventions and innovations have not entered society at random, shedding their advantages or disadvantages indifferently over all industries or individuals. On the contrary, I believe that technology enters our kind of society in a systematic fashion, and that there is a discoverable pattern behind its appearance, now in this area of social effort, and now in that particular area.

Very simply, the pattern is due to the enormous magnetic pull exerted by an existing economic structure on the minds of men who are concerned with making and applying inventions and innovations. There is, of course, a large element of freedom, of chance, of individual adventure, in the advance of scientific understanding. But when it comes to the incorporation of the existing body of scientific knowledge into daily work in a society activated by private gain, I suspect that attention and effort will naturally be concentrated on those tasks and challenges that predominate at a given time. To put it as concretely as possible, I imagine that in a largely agricultural society, the focus of technical inventiveness would naturally fall on agricultural processes, that in a society turning toward industrialism, the focus would be spontaneously directed toward machines having to do with manufacture, etc. Needless to say, the pace and direction of technological change will be powerfully influenced by other factors, such as the relative dearness of labor or capital; but, other things equal, as the economist says, I would think that the changing nature of the social task itself will serve as a major guide.

Is this proposition empirically demonstrable? Here our woeful lack of systematic knowledge begins to get in our way. Yet I think one can discern a grand sequence of inventive endeavor in the United States, with, needless to say, many overlaps and anachronisms. The sequence begins, chronologically as well as in terms of concentration of effort, with agriculture. For all the early improvements in textile machinery, or the introduction of railroads and steamships, I think it is fair to say that the sector of the economy that initially experienced the grand impulse of technology was basic farming. First the epochal cotton gin, then the iron plow, the harrow and the seed drill, then the mechanical reaper, and all along the way the gradual substitution of horsepower for manpower — taken in its entirety, this was nothing less than a technological revolution which was in full force by the 1860's. It was not only the quality, but the quantity of capital, that worked its dynamic effect. By 1900 more money was invested in the reaper than in any other machine in the world save only the steam engine, and by 1960 the average worker in agriculture employed more capital ($21,300) than the average worker in manufacturing ($15,900).

The table below[1] gives us some idea of the enormous increase in the productivity of farm labor that resulted from this revolution:

MAN-HOUR REQUIREMENTS PER ACRE

	1800	1840	1880	1920	1960
corn	86	69	46	33	10
wheat	56	35	20	12	4
cotton	185	135	119	96	66

The statistics clearly bespeak the long history of agricultural improvement. By contrast, in the field of manufacturing — or rather, in that congeries of tasks associated with handling, shaping, assembling, processing and transporting goods — the main entrance of technology begins rather later, around the time of the

---

[1] W. D. Rasmussen, "The Impact of Technological Change on American Agriculture," *Journal of Economic History* (December 1962).

Civil War. As late as 1869, for instance, nearly half of the mechanical power in manufacturing still came from water wheels rather than steam engines. Although immensely important inventions and improvements begin to revolutionize some aspects of manufacturing early in the 19th century, the great transformation of industrial production does not gain momentum until the latter half of the 19th century, reaching its climax in the mass production techniques of the 20th century.

There is an important consequence to this wave-like succession of technological salients of advance. It is that the productivity of all workers in all sectors and echelons does not rise straight across the board, like a well-drilled parade of soldiers, but changes in uneven fashion as different areas of work are successively affected by technology.

We have already seen the improvement in agricultural man-hour productivity which we could trace back to the beginning of the 19th century. The statistics of manufacturing are less satisfactory, partly of course because many of the manufacturing processes do not extend as far back in time as do basic agricultural tasks. Hence in following the general trend of manufacturing productivity somewhat more impressionistic estimates have to suffice. We know, for instance, that a man in a pulp and paper plant in the late 1950's produced about three times as much output in an hour as did his predecessor after World War I; that a worker in a steel plant over the same period quadrupled his hourly output of steel; that a worker in a cigarette factory increased his or her production by six times. Taking "manufactures" generally, it is usually estimated that an average worker today produces about five or six times as much, per unit of time, as did his great-great-grandfather at the time of the Civil War.

Impact on Productivity

To these essentially familar statistics we must now add a third set of figures having to do with the impact of technology on productivity — or rather, in the absence of reliable statistics, we must add our impressions as to what the figures would be if they existed. These concern a group of occupations distinct from those of farm and "factory," that we will label "office" and "service" work, meaning by this a wide variety of jobs that administer, supervise, service, instruct and cater to society.

Some of these employments, and the roughly-estimated numbers of people who are engaged in them can be seen below:

"OFFICE" AND "SERVICE" OCCUPATIONS, 1962

Teachers, incl. college	1,900,000
Salesmen and salesclerks	3,700,000
Nonfarm managers and proprietors	5,400,000
Bookkeepers	900,000
Waiters, waitresses, kitchen help (not private household)	1,100,000
Cooks (not private household)	600,000
Protective service workers	700,000
Clergymen	200,000
Lawyers	200,000
Doctors and dentists	300,000
Hospital attendants	400,000
Cashiers	500,000
Secretaries, stenos, typists	2,300,000
Nurses	600,000

This is of course only a sampling of the various kinds of activities I have in mind. I have omitted 100,000 editors and reporters, 300,000 musicians, 100,000 social workers, 350,000 insurance agents, 200,000 newsboys, and so on. In all, perhaps 35 million people have some kind of nonfarm, nonfactory public or private job.

Whatever shortages of data troubled us before vex us to an even higher degree here. By and large there are no estimates of the increased productivity of clerks and barbers, administrators and janitors over the years. Hence we are perforce reduced to very uncertain evidence when we try to measure the impact of technology on this last group of occupations. But the overwhelming — and I think trustworthy — impression one gets is that the manhour productivity of these jobs has not risen to anything like the extent of improvement in farm and "factory" work.

There are, to be sure, technological changes that have appreciably — even very greatly — raised the level of particular office employments. One thinks of the plane and the automobile that have added cubits to the stature of the traveling salesman, the telephone that has vastly extended the productivity of all supervisory tasks, the office adding machine that has helped the bookkeeper, and the indispensable typewriter. These improvements notwithstanding, one cannot easily establish a steady upward march of productivity in the office as one does in the factory. Manhour productivity indices for "distribution," for instance, show a rise of only one-sixth that of manufacturing between 1900 and 1929. Many occupations — waiters, for instance — are virtually the same today as a hundred years ago, not to say worse. And as every businessman will testify, what eats up costs these days is not so much production as "overhead." What this means, of course, is that technology has not yet entered the "office" to nearly the degree that it has overrun farm and factory.

An Important Generalization

We will return shortly to the significance of this laggard area of technological advance. First, however, we must add an important economic generalization to our general historic schema. It is that the impact of technology on output, when it is introduced into a new industry or sector, is not alone determined by the new physical capabilities of production stemming from the new techniques. Rather, it is determined by the interplay of these new capabilities with the stern economic realities of demand.

An illustration may make this clearer. Suppose we have an industry producing, let us say, clothespins. Presumably it is already producing as many clothespins with its existing techniques as consumers will buy at going prices. Now suppose that a technological improvement doubles the productivity of each man, thereby halving the cost of clothespins (we will forget about the cost of the new machines). Clearly, unless sales increase we will not be able to employ the former labor force. But will sales increase? That hinges entirely on the response — or "elasticity" — of demand when clothespin prices are now cut. If clothespin prices are cut in half and as a result consumers buy three times as many pins as before, employment in the industry will rise. But if they only buy 50 percent more than before the price cut, employment will fall.

This little excursion into elementary economics is necessary if we are now to proceed from our general discussion of technological entry to its effect on employment. For everything, it must now be clear, depends on the responsiveness of demand for the various kinds of goods that technology makes available. In the case of farm products, for instance, demand has always been notoriously *in*elastic — that is, very unresponsive to price cuts. Hence as agricultural output steadily expanded throughout the 19th century, it met a wall of consumer indifference. The desire to buy wheat and corn at prevailing prices did not by any matter of means keep pace with the enlarged capacity to produce them, with the result that employment on the farm fell precipitously. At the beginning of the 19th century perhaps 75 or 80 percent of the labor force was engaged in farm tasks. By the end of the century this had been cut to 30 percent. By mid-20th century it was down to 8 percent.

Thus the entry of technology into a sector where demand was relatively unresponsive forced an exodus of labor into other areas — which is to say, into the city and its "factory" jobs. And fortunately, at least in the beginning and middle of the 19th century, the demand for factory products was much more elastic than that for farm goods. Even though individual productivity was steadily rising in "factory" work throughout the 19th century, particularly after the Civil War, the demand for manufactured and processed goods was sufficiently buoyant so that employment could also steadily expand. In the year 1800 "factory" occupations accounted for perhaps only 5 to 10 percent of the nation's labor distribution, but by 1900 they constituted a full 37 percent.

Thereafter, a somewhat different constellation of forces seems to have prevailed. Perhaps the elasticity of consumer demand for further manufactures began to fall; perhaps the productivity of "factory" work rose at an accelerated rate. Whatever the cause, the percentage of the nation's work force engaged in "factory" jobs remained fairly constant. By 1960 only 39 percent of the labor force was in manufacturing, mining, transportation, utilities, construction, etc., compared with the 37 percent at the turn of the century. And this much more sluggish rate of growth is given further significance when we recall that weekly hours of work had been reduced from 60 in 1900 to 40 in 1960. Were it not for this fall in hours of work per week — in other words, had we combined the new technology with workmen who labored the long week of the 1900's — the volume of employment needed to satisfy the demands for "factory" goods would have fallen sharply. Indeed, from 1957 to 1962, despite rising output, there *was* a steady gradual shrinkage of 100,000 jobs in manufacturing, and whereas this trend has recently been reversed, there continues to be a fall in employment in mining and utilities.

Meanwhile, what of the labor that was inexorably being pushed off the farm all through the 20th century? Since the growth of "factory" occupations was slowing down, clearly employment had to be provided on some other front. And so it was, by the wide range of "office" and "service" jobs we have already noticed. Here, not only was demand elastic for the services they performed but — and this is the crucial point of the whole analysis — the productivity of these occupations had not risen greatly. As a result, the rising demand for the output of "office work" resulted in a very large rise in the number of people hired to perform this work. In 1900 only a quarter of the labor force was in the spectrum of the service, administrative and other functions embraced by this last sector of employment. By 1965 over 50 percent of the labor force had entered these jobs, thanks mainly to the fact that technology had not yet duplicated their tasks as it had in farm and factory labor.

A New Turn for Technology

So much by way of background. I move now to a suggestion that may put the problem of automation into the perspective of theory and history that we have sought. It is that technology is belatedly gathering momentum in the direction of "office" and "service" tasks, thereby invading those sheltered precincts of the economy in which labor has not yet been exposed to the full competition of machinery.

My suggestion — it cannot be more than that until we know more about the nature of contemporary technology and its points of application throughout the economy — puts the concern about "automation" into a somewhat different focus than is customary. Ben Seligman, for example, in *Dissent* (Winter, 1965) lists an impressive number of instances where the new technology of computers, feedback systems, sensory equipment, etc., has displaced labor, much of it "factory" labor. I do not question the validity of his instances, but I do question whether dollar for dollar this new factory equipment is any more labor-displacing than "old-fashioned" equipment such as fork-lift trucks, overhead conveyors, high-speed machinery, and so on. I must confess that I can neither see any reason *a priori* why a dollar's worth of "automation" equipment should replace any more labor than a dollar's worth of less fancy mechanical equipment, nor can I, as yet, find any statistical evidence that manufacturing productivity is rising faster today than over a number of periods in the past — for instance, from 1920 to 1924.

In other words, I do not see the threat of automation in any unusual characteristics possessed by modern day "factory" technology. What I *do* suspect, on the other hand, is that the new technology is threatening a whole new group of skills — the sorting, filing, checking, calculating, remembering, comparing, okaying skills — that are the special preserve of the office worker. Moreover, it is not just complicated computers that are threatening to take over functions in this hitherto sheltered area of work, although no doubt the new technology is conducive to more complex administrative tasks. Very simple machines may also invade the field — vending machines, or organizational innovations such as discount houses, or zip code numbers that speed mail sorting. To put it differently, it seems to me that office and service work is now the area that cries out to be rationalized, simplified, and abridged by machinery, just as did farm work in the early 1800's and factory work later in the 19th century. In an economy where effort usually follows incentive, it would be unusual if technology did not turn in this beckoning direction.

Factors Affecting Employment

How severe a challenge does this pose to the economic system? The answer, if we assume that technology is in fact moving in the direction I suggest, is not a simple one. It will depend on the conjunctions of many forces which buffer or aggravate the displacement effect of technology alone.

One aggravating factor will be the growth in the labor supply itself. Each year sees a small but significant increase in the number of married women looking for work, whether lured by the prospect of a two-income household, by the lessened chores of housework, or by "The Feminine Mystique." Even more important will be the coming-of-age of the bumper crops of war babies, now about to graduate from high school and college. All in all, the number of job-seekers is slated to rise alarmingly over the coming years. From 1947 to 1957 the number of people within the "working-age" brackets of 15 to 65 increased by 8.3 million. In the six years between 1964 and 1970 it will rise by nearly *fifteen* million. Thus the changing composition of the labor force will crowd the labor markets and intensify the struggle for jobs (and the failure-rate in finding jobs) for reasons having nothing to do with automation.

A second factor bearing on unemployment is our over-all rate of economic expansion. In *The Price of Prosperity,* Peter Bernstein has reminded us that our current rate of economic growth of about 4 percent a year is a third higher than our long-run "secular" rate of growth. He points out that even if the work week is cut to 37.5 hours, and if technological improvements come no faster than in the recent past, our unemployment could reach 10 million people by 1970, should our rate of growth fall back to the "norm" of 3 percent. It might even touch 15 millions, if the rate reverted to the 2.5 percent growth figure of the 1957-1960 era.

The remedy, says Bernstein and most other economists, is to use every device to make sure that our growth does not slacken, but rather increases. But the matter is not quite so simple as that. For if our rate of growth is accelerated by a burst of labor-saving technology, we could experience both a higher rate of output *and* a higher rate of unemployment. There is, of course, always the chance and the hope that our growth could be hastened by the emergence of a great new employment-generating industry, comparable to the auto industry in the 1910's and 1920's. All one can say, when this possibility is raised, is that such an industry is not now visible, and that expansion in private output since World War II — impressive both in volume and in new kinds of goods — has not been very conducive to an expansion of employment. According to no less an authority than Secretary of Labor Willard Wirtz, of the 4 million new full-time jobs created between 1947 and 1963, *only 5 percent* originated in the private sector.

Shortening the Work Week?

There remains another general solution, largely advocated by the labor movement — the contraction of the work week. The rationale is simple and incontestable. By shortening the work week (through the imposition of overtime rates after, say, 30 hours of work), employers are induced to spread the existing volume of work among more people. Or they may simply throttle back their output to 30 hours, thereby making it more attractive for a new plant to be built to cater to the market.

There can be no doubt that the shortening of the work week has been a principal method of absorbing the "surplus productivity" of machines, and there can be no doubt that it will continue to constitute a main avenue of social adjustment. After all, the whole purpose of the introduction of technology is to enable men to work less hard, or at least to enable them to transfer their labor from unpleasant to pleasant tasks. The trouble with adjustments in hours is that they require the cooperation of labor as regards the cost of the new shorter work week. If we suppose that the work week were suddenly reduced to 20 hours, we can easily see that employers would be willing to hire twice as many workers as they now have — provided that the men who did the first twenty hours of work did not demand as much as pay as they formerly got for 40 hours.

The adjustment of the work week, in other words, depends on how much of a cut in wages (if any) labor is willing to take, and on how a rise in labor costs will affect employers' willingness to expand their work forces (or intensify their search for labor-saving machinery). It is impossible to make firm predictions about any side of this problem, other than that the issue itself is not likely to be rapidly resolved. Ten or twenty years from now we may have eased ourselves into a "normal" work week of 30 or even fewer hours, but during the next crucial decade it seems fruitless to look to this source for a major alleviation of the unemployment issue.

This seems to leave, as the main buffering force during those

years, and indeed for many years thereafter, the deliberate use of
public employment-generating or spreading policies. There are a
number of possibilities that might be tried. For instance, the government could try to reduce the number of people looking for work
by subsidizing young people to remain in school and college. Another policy along similar lines would encourage earlier voluntary
retirement by lowering the Social Security retirement age and rais-
ing benefits. A much more drastic course would be the use of dis-
criminatory taxation against two income families to hold back the
growth of the female labor force, although this would be harder to
defend on social grounds. Turning the coin over, it should also be
possible for government to create employment in the private sector
— for instance, by giving tax benefits to employers who expand
their labor forces, or in certain carefully controlled situations by
permitting a reduction of the minimum wage, paying the lost income differential directly to the employees concerned.

Finding New Employments

But I suspect that the main line of defense against unemployment, whether caused by the incursion of technology or by the burgeoning of the labor force, will have to come from a different direction. What is needed above all is a new expansive group of employments to offer the same absorptive cushion once given by office and
service jobs. And if this is the objective, it is not difficult to know
where to look to find such employments. We have merely to ask
ourselves: what tasks in society are clearly and admittedly under-
manned? The answer is provided by every city, in its shortage of
adequate housing, its unbeautified and ill-maintained streets and
parks, its under-protected citizens, under-educated children, under-
cared-for young and old and sick. The trouble is, of course, that
all these employments, the need for which seems incontestable, require for their realization vast new funds for the public or private
philanthropic agencies if they are to be tomorrow's employers of
today's unemployed. If those funds are to be sufficient to rebuild
the warrens of our cities, and to offer good work to the five to ten
million who seem the minimum number of the otherwise unemployed, what is needed is nothing less than a whole new attitude

toward the appropriate public-private mix for the peacetime economy.

There will be difficulty enough in creating such a new attitude in time to meet the onrush of technology and the pressure of the growing labor force. Yet in this essay that covers so much ground, albeit so casually, it must be admitted that even this necessary redirection of social effort is only a palliative. In the end, as machines continue to invade society, duplicating greater and greater numbers of social tasks, it is human labor itself — at least, as we now think of "labor" — that is gradually rendered redundant. The underworld of economic thought, where wish and fantasy often take the place of thought and fact, is nonetheless right in its basic premonitions. The machine does challenge man, mechanical energies do replace human energies, the harnessing of nature does imply the releasing of humanity. The question is — and it is not too early to ask it, even though the answers be only visions for the future — for what is it to be released?

C. Commentary and Analysis

The first impression we have when reflecting upon Heilbroner's article is the vastness of the economic effect upon the world of work. The economist today, at least the theoretical economist, must be concerned with the total world of work, for he sees how interlaced are the different kinds of work and business, within and among communities, within and among nations. It is clear to the economist that for any individual person, corporation or nation to assess its own economic health and growth, it must concern itself with the world of work. For example, Heilbroner compares the effects of automation on three classes of work: farm, factory and clerical-service work. He showed how the three types are interrelated in the economic world, how problems and solutions in one area are going to cause problems and, hopefully, solutions in another area. And all of this happens within a worldwide context.

The point for our Christian reflection here is simply this, that we too must acknowledge that *our* work as well as that of our family and nation fits into a world picture. We see through Heilbroner's article and the other readings suggested at the conclusion of this book that in many ways economics and mutual economic interdependence on an ever larger scale has brought about precisely a *world* of work. The Christian today must understand that he works, not for himself or for a single business enterprise, but within a nation of workers in a world of work. We must learn as Christians to think "world," to put ourselves and our careers and occupations from time to time within a universal perspective, to think in terms of mankind and not always merely in terms of our biological families or, worse, ourselves.

There are of course many problems on the individual and work-group levels which come to light because of unhappy economic situations. No one would dare deny the painful effects of unemployment or unfair labor practices, child labor, and so forth. But, at this point, without making little of these special problems, it seems more profitable to turn our reflection on the economic world toward the vision it offers of the "big picture," which tells us where we as mankind have progressed from, where we are today in the world of work, and where we are headed for in the future. All three viewpoints are essential for a true Christian vision of mankind. For if man in his interaction with his fellowmen and the world is moving *somewhere, somehow,* this goal should be important to the Christian, especially since it should influence the way he reacts and responds to his task in the world of work.

Economics is one area, one dimension which reflects clearly the revolutionary changes in the character of humanity's creative advances. The three simple steps of *knowledge* leading to *control* leading to *power* in the history of finance, technology, and the biological and social sciences teach us much concerning the growth of the human community. Not only is the solidarity of mankind re-emphasized, but growth in the community of persons through the communion of "goods" — information, inventions, objects, experience — all this has brought us to a deeper understanding of love for the created world.

To reflect on the communion of goods in the natural order is to realize that life consists in exchanges. And through reflection on our world of work we see the universal extension of these "exchanges." Whatever science acquires, whatever understanding or agreement the United Nations reaches, affects the whole of mankind. We are in a world of exchanges. This international communion is more pronounced when the events involve evil consequences, such as in wars, famines, economic depressions.

However, the communion of goods founded on the Christian life of grace invites us, not to disregard evil, but to strive to overcome it. For, says Abbé Roger Hasseveldt, "the divine life is one of exchange. The Trinity is formed by the mutual exchange of the three Persons. Each Person exists only in order to give himself and by giving himself." [2]

Hence, since we share this divine life in Christ, our lives are essentially lives of self-giving or exchange. But, seeing the importance and integrality of the world of work and created goods in human development, we must recognize that essential to our mutual exchange of selves in love, there is an exchange of material goods within our human endeavor. Much of our love is expressed through deeds and work in and with matter.

Creation hidden full with potentialities as a gift from God is a sign of his love coming to us through the world of matter. How better to show our appreciation than to use the gift, this gift that mysteriously sometimes leads us away from a love of gratitude to a love of selfishness and possessiveness, but which still more mysteriously often brings mankind into a solidarity of union and potential for deeper love and communion. It is this latter drive for solidarity that we wish to focus upon, this positive movement of mankind.

In order to act responsibly toward material creation, we must strive to see it in its completeness. This once again is the lesson of the economist. Completeness demands that we recognize the potential of the present as accurately as we can to better see the vision of the future. The two poles of understanding, the present and the future, are essential for the effective progress of mankind, for its positive movement. To see the present is to evaluate the

---

[2] *The Church: A Divine Mystery,* tr. William Storey (Chicago: Fides, 1954), p. 27.

store of knowledge and abilities we have, to assess the state of things, the needs and the difficulties of the contemporary scene. After all, progress is really a product, an end result. The present is a product of the past. And if there is to be an ever richer product in the future, the meaning of work and human endeavor in the created world must be continually re-evaluated in terms of today.

The vision of the future is also necessary. Goals, vague as they often are, still are a necessary element of human progress. Surprises are pleasant at times. But for the most part people prefer to know what to expect. Heilbroner tells us that we can expect to see automation entering into the clerical world on a grand scale in the near future. Schneider in his study of the family and industry predicted directions which the form and function of the family in modern society will take. Trent and his colleagues hint at some of the changes likely to occur in the structure and content of the educational world. Montessori tells us of the potentialities opening up in human development through the maximum utilization of the "sensitive periods" in the maturation process of the person. Brown points to the improvement in understanding the motivational behavior of formal and informal groups in the work setting discovered by the social psychologists.

All of these insights of the social scientists help the Christian in his vision of the future of man. Furthermore, they help him in a very practical way, far more than the abstract reflections of the philosopher. For today the Christian must not only philosophize about the future, he must create it. He is responsible to God for the world. His responsibility includes the many concrete ethical problems presented by automation, but it also includes the vision of the future and the kingdom. And from the vision of the future, the Christian thinker must learn to see how automation presents problems and possibilities which are beyond ethics.

From another point of view, Heilbroner pointed out that there are some problems which society avoids and often refuses to admit. Perhaps the response here demands Christians imbued with the optimism of the earth and the optimism of the resurrection. When imbued with the optimism of the earth, the Christian will have the eager willingness to face the problems which society avoids; and when in addition the Christian is imbued with the optimism of the resurrection, he will have the vision to see the bright possibilities of the future and an approach to solutions for the avoided problems. And here for the Christian the "changing nature of the social task itself will serve as a major guide."

Questions for Discussion

1. What does socio-economic growth and survival demand today? What is the significance of technology here?
2. What has been the impact of the long neglect of technology as a labor-displacing force? How does Heilbroner illustrate his idea that technology enters contemporary society in a systematic fashion? What is an important consequence of this?
3. Explain the interplay between capabilities of production and elasticity in consumer demands. Why is this interplay important? How does it affect employment?
4. What areas of work does Heilbroner see as suddenly feeling the fuller impact of automation? How severe a challenge does he find this? What tasks are not being accomplished in society today?
5. What lessons can the economist teach the Christian?

IX
WORK AND THE
CREATIVE PERSON

A. Prenote

In a society where novelty and newness are among the supreme values, the creative person is desperately needed. Corporations employ armies of people who do nothing but plan, think, predict, invent, create. In the world of work today the creative person is crucial. And although the personality of the creative individual is not characteristically well-rounded, as psychologists' tests report, nevertheless the large corporation welcomes him, for the creative person is one of the very few sources whereby the productive organization can stay youthful and grow.

The fact that the corporations are in search of creative people does not deny the need for creativity in the art world. Painting, music, sculpture, and the rest of the fields of interest concerned with aesthetics have traditionally been the domain of creativity. The work of the artist is synonymous with creativity. But today the career of the artist has been modified; not even his creativity has escaped the influence of technology and the secularized world.

In this chapter Helen Rowan, writing for *Think* (November 1962), points out that creativity in general does not flourish in our present sociocultural climate, and yet by all indications it seems that the survival of human life as a whole "depends upon the ability and the disposition of human beings to think original thoughts."

B: Selection: The Creative People: How To Spot Them[1]

Probably everybody has some of it; almost everybody wants more of it; and nobody knows exactly how to go about getting it.

The desired commodity is "creativity." The word appears with increasing frequency in the popular as well as the esoteric press of the land. Seminars are held on creativity. Ways of inculcating creativeness are sought by parent-teacher organizations and management groups. The mother who in the 1930's wanted her child to be nothing so much as "adjusted" now wishes him to be, above all things, "creative." From teachers and businessmen, parents and government officials come pleas for more creativity.

Whether the genuinely creative person is as a matter of fact *welcome* in home or classroom, business office or laboratory is quite another story, which we can sidestep for the moment. For before we can even speculate profitably about that question we must have answers to the more basic ones: What is the creative person like? Are there traits of personality that set him off from less creative people? Does he do his thinking in a different way? How does he create?

The most intensive and at the same time wide-ranging research into the personality characteristics of creative individuals has been made in the course of a seven-year-long study conducted by the University of California's Institute of Personality Assessment and Research (IPAR) under the leadership of Donald W. MacKinnon. Many of IPAR's findings are supported, whether explicitly or implicitly, by the findings of other social scientists.

What IPAR did was to study hundreds of creative individuals in a variety of fields. The basic questions IPAR wanted to answer were: How do the creatives differ among themselves and how do all of them differ from all of us?

The individuals IPAR studied included creative writers, research scientists and mathematicians, and architects. These groups were chosen as representing what the IPAR people believe are three somewhat different types of creativity.

Three Creative Types

The first type is exemplified by creative writers and other kinds of artists. A novelist or poet may write for the purpose of making money, but what he produces is clearly a reflection of his inner state; his creative product is not the result of an outside definition. In the second type of creativity, however, which is represented in the IPAR sample by mathematicians and scientists, the individual is acting largely to meet externally defined needs and goals. It becomes apparent, for example, that a theory is necessary to explain a certain natural phenomenon. The Einstein who produces such a theory has certainly created an original and appropriate product, but it is not "himself" in the sense that a Mozart symphony is Mozart.

And then there is a third type of creativity which cuts across the other two: architects, as well as those in other groups, demonstrate this type of creativity. The architect is told to build a school or a church, for example, capable of holding so many people, on this certain plot of land, and so on. In that sense he is certainly acting to meet "externally defined needs and goals." But what he produces in response to those needs is an expression of himself, and hence a very personal product.

All of the individuals studied had been nominated as creative by eminent persons in their own field.

In trying to learn what creative people are like, IPAR used a method of personality assessment developed by the Office of Strategic Services during World War II for screening personnel for risky jobs in occupied areas. The method — a long-drawn-out one — involves giving a large number of tests of aptitudes, values and interests, etc., conducting long interviews, and observing the individuals under different circumstances. From all of these tests, interviews and observations a picture of the person, as a whole, emerges.

How do creative people, as a whole, look?

Certain adjectives immediately spring to mind. Independent is certainly one of them — perhaps the first. Original is another. Flexible. Open. Nonauthoritarian. Sensitive, in a certain meaning of the word. Playful — of all things. Intuitive. Energetic.

And intelligent. Let's start with that characteristic. Highly creative people are highly intelligent, but the obverse is not necessarily true. That is, highly intelligent people are not highly creative, as a moment's thought about one's own personal acquaintances will make clear.

IPAR found that all the creative individuals it studied were intelligent, but that above a certain level — perhaps 120 as measured on standard IQ tests — there was no significant correlation between intelligence and the degree of creativity shown. Many other psychologists have commented on this lack of relationship, and some of them suggest that our intelligence tests not only do not measure creativity (which, it should be remembered, the makers of the tests do not claim they do) but also that they do not measure certain *kinds* of cognitive ability.

IQ and Creativity

In research done with children in a Midwestern school, Jacob W. Getzels and Philip W. Jackson of the University of Chicago selected two groups, one highly intelligent when measured by IQ but not highly creative, the other highly creative but not as highly intelligent when measured by IQ. The highly intelligent group had an average IQ 23 points higher than the creative group. Yet these highly creative children did as well in academic achievement as measured by standardized achievement tests as did the high IQ children. And this result cannot, perhaps unfortunately, be explained in terms of the teachers' fondness for the highly creative pupils, because a searching examination of the teachers' attitudes revealed that although they preferred teaching high IQ children rather than average children, they did *not* show a similar preference for the highly creative. (The reasons for this will become obvious when we look at the characteristics of temperament of creative individuals.) Getzels and Jackson infer that highly creative children have some cognitive abilities that the IQ tests do not test.

Two Kinds Of Thinking

Other pieces of the intelligence-creativity puzzle are furnished by the work of J. P. Guilford of the University of Southern California. Guilford describes two kinds of thinking; convergent and divergent.

Convergent thinking demands the ability to recognize, to remember, to solve by moving toward one right answer or some one answer that is more or less clearly called for. The intellectual abilities required for this kind of thinking are chiefly what the intelligence test measures.

But divergent thinking emphasizes searching activities, with the freedom to think in different directions; it may call for the ability to invent or innovate. It is this kind of thinking, Guilford and others believe, that is a hallmark of the creative person's intellect; but standard tests do not measure the quality to any significant degree.

Guilford also isolates certain aptitude traits that he believes are related to creativity. He lists the ability to see problems — to see gaps between what is and what could or should be. He mentions fluency — of words, of associations, of expressions, of ideas. He of course mentions originality. He notices the ability of creative individuals to redefine—to improvise, to use familar facts or objects in new ways. And he sees their ability to elaborate — to construct from a simple foundation a more elaborate structure.

It is interesting to note here that *non*intellectual traits—characteristics of temperament and motivation — of highly creative individuals also play a powerful role. This is strikingly epitomized in a case uncovered by MacKinnon and his group at IPAR.

At one point, they made a study of spare-time inventors. The most inventive of their inventors turned up with a score of exactly *six* on the Terman Concept Mastery Test. This test, while emphasizing verbal abilities, is considered to have a strong positive correlation to general intelligence. The writers IPAR studied averaged 156 on it; the scientists were near 120.

The test is scored by subtracting the number of wrong answers from the number right. When the inventive inventor's test was analyzed, it showed that if his right answers alone had been considered, he would have scored a perfectly respectable 87. As MacKinnon points out, that man was more than willing to impart any information he had in his head, including wrong information or hunches. One has to look to qualities other than mere intelligence to explain his score: intellectual energy, the willingness to try anything, lack of fear of being wrong, the bent toward innovation. And it is presumably those qualities that make him a productive inventor.

In differing degrees, those characteristics just mentioned, along with a number of others, seem to mark all highly creative people. In fact, what is striking is the extraordinary degree to which certain qualities are shared by *all* creative types, whether mathematicians or artists, architects or writers. There are certain sharp differences but they may be readily explained in terms of different types of creativity, and are so few that it makes sense to discuss them first.

The vast majority of mathematicians, for example, are introverted, while writers are as likely to be extroverted as introverted. But this is not surprising. The writer is concerned with "outer" as well as "inner" weather, to paraphrase Robert Frost. In thinking, mathematicians and scientists tend to be *judgmental* — to come to a conclusion about something; while writers are *perceptive,* being more interested simply in knowing what the world is like rather than judging it. And in the contrast between thinking and feeling as modes of judging and evaluating experience, scientists and mathematicians are strongly "thinking" types, while writers are just as strongly "feeling." Architects split down the middle.

Overwhelming Intuition

The qualities that unite creative individuals, however, are both more numerous and more important than those that divide them. The qualities they share have to do with their interests, values and a number of tendencies that might be summed up under "style," for want of a better word: *a general openness to experience from both without and within; a toleration for ambiguity, confusion and disorder; the strong disposition to be independent rather than conforming; and the tendency to perceive through intuition rather than the senses.*

In fact, this strongly intuitive quality, which the creatives show almost unanimously, separates them most sharply and dramatically from the average. In the general population, three out of every four persons are sense perceptives. They concentrate on things presented to their five senses, and they focus their attention upon existing *facts.* The one out of every four who perceives intuitively focuses upon *possibilities;* he looks expectantly for a link between something present and something not yet thought of.

Highly creative people in all fields are overwhelmingly intuitive. We would not expect them to be bound by what *is;* we would expect them to be alert to, to be seeking, what *could be.* But the fact that almost a hundred percent of them are so, as contrasted with only 25 percent of the general population, is an impressive and important finding.

In the matter of interests, all the creative individuals in the IPAR studies, no matter what their own calling, scored high on interests which might lead them to become psychologists, architects, author-journalists. All scored low on scales for office workers, bankers, farmers, policemen.

The conclusion to draw from this finding is not that no bankers or farmers are creative, which does not follow, but rather that highly creative individuals are not very much interested in small detail, in the practical and concrete, at least in matters outside their own field. They are more concerned with the meanings, implications and symbolic equivalents of things. This finding is not very surprising, and many other signs support its validity.

A finding which *is* more surprising has to do with the values creative individuals share. The German psychologist Eduard Spranger has described six basic values of men as being: the aesthetic, economic, political, social, religious and theoretical.

For all the creative types the aesthetic and the theoretical are the strongest; the economic is often the weakest. This should be of special interest to the employers of creative workers, for it suggests a basic difference, if not conflict of values between business-men and the employees they hire to be creative. It may explain the frequent lack of understanding between them.

That the economic value is lowest is not surprising, however, given what we know about the interests and preferences of highly creative persons. But what does or did surprise psychologists, until they thought longer about it, is that the two values that are usually considered to be conflicting — the theoretical and the aesthetic — are so high and of so nearly the same strength for all creative groups.

They Resolve the Conflict

Highly creative people rise above the seeming conflict between theoretical and aesthetic values or — closer to the truth — *resolve* it. They are more able than most to give expression to opposite sides of their nature, to achieve a reconciliation of the conscious and unconscious, reason and passion, rational and irrational, science and art.

It is this quality of openness, of lack of rigidity, that seems a particularly strong mark of all creative types.

On certain tests, for example, all the highly creative male groups IPAR studied scored high on traits which in our culture are considered "feminine." They were more open in their feelings and emotions, more sensitively aware of themselves and others, interested in a wide range of matters. Yet most of them were not effeminate in manner or appearance, but instead assertive, dominant and self-confident.

Creative individuals also seem to have a positive preference for complexity. When presented with a series of designs of various types they consistently choose those which are more abstract, perhaps chaotic; when offered an opportunity to make mosaic patterns using many or few colors, the highly creative tend to employ more colors, the less creative fewer. It seems that the less creative person has to impose order immediately, but that the more creative sees the possibility of imposing a higher level of order, having previously experienced more disorder. Here, too, the aesthetic-theoretical relationship comes in, as illustrated by the mathematician who will ignore certain obvious solutions to a problem in favor of an "elegant" or beautiful one.

Playing with Ideas

Guilford, too, mentions toleration of ambiguity among the non-intellectual traits shown by the creative individuals he has studied. And New York University psychologist Morris I. Stein, who has studied research chemists over a number of years, says the creative ones are less rigid, less authoritarian, and like to "play" with ideas.

Frank Barron of IPAR gives a good summing up of all this by saying, "The creative person is both more primitive and more cultivated, more destructive and more constructive, a lot madder and a lot saner, than the average person. "

To be all those things at once the human being must have a strong ego, and this is indeed a distinguishing characteristic of the creative type. The highly creative individual possesses a self-confidence that amounts almost to a sense of destiny, and has a strong commitment to his goal.

The picture thus drawn is of a highly independent person. And that, of course, is what a highly creative person is. Now we may also describe him in terms of what he is *not*.

First and foremost, he is not a conformist. As Nevitt Sanford of Stanford asks, "How can anyone think original thoughts if he is disposed to think what others are thinking?"

Most highly creative individuals, however, despite the popular stereotype of them, do not waste their time and energy in "non-conforming" to the trivia of social convention. In fact, the IPAR group remarked on what they call the "briefcase syndrome" among many creative individuals. They tend to marry only one woman (at a time), and wear neckties to funerals. It is in the deeper world—of ideas and thinking — that the independent person is a nonconformist; in fact, it appears that many creative people are conventional in ways that facilitate life in the group precisely so that they may be left unhindered to pursue their own deeper aims.

Richard Crutchfield of IPAR says, "The truly independent person — in whom creative thinking is at its best — is someone who can accept society without denying himself."

The fact is, however, that human beings being what they are, and American society in the 20th century being what it is, many in accepting society *do* deny themselves. And in so doing they are denying their own potentialities for creativity; for the characteristics that go with conforming behavior correlate negatively with virtually every one of the numerous measures of originality used by IPAR (and others, for that matter).

Crutchfield mentions the following characteristics of individuals who tend toward conforming behavior, as compared with those of independent behavior. They are less intelligent, are rigid in their thinking, and are relatively impoverished in the realm of ideas. They are lower in ego-strength and the ability to cope with stress, and repress many of their impulses. They have more feeling of personal inferiority and lack of self-confidence. They are far more conventional and moralistic, and these tendencies are often coupled with an authoritarian outlook.

A Special Freedom

"Freedom" is the word that seems to sum up what the creative individual most needs — or rather what the truly creative individual manages to achieve for himself. Freedom to be himself, to acknowledge his own impulses, to believe his own vision of the world, to set his own goals, to establish his own hierarchy of values. This freedom does not mean license. In fact, the goals the creative person sets for himself are probably far higher than those anyone else would think of setting for him; the demands he makes of himself are more rigorous than those that anyone would or could make of him. Nevertheless it is in pursuit of this kind of freedom that the creative person most often comes into open or covert, subtle or sharp conflict with "the group."

Young Rebels

It is a fact, for example, that many highly creative adults did not "do well" in school. Most often it is not that they were openly rebellious — though some were — but rather that in vigorous pursuit of their own goals they declined to seek the goals set for the class. This tendency toward independent goal-setting is noticed in the Getzels and Jackson study of children who are believed to be creative (although, of course, only time will tell if they prove to be), and it is often carried all the way through college and beyond. Many of the most highly creative architects did brilliantly in certain college courses, but did not bother to do anything in (or even attend) other courses that did not interest them. And even in his home the creative child may not be a "satisfactory member of the family group," preferring to follow his own interests most of the time, and sometimes craving solitude.

If all of this seems to add up to a picture of someone who is not "well-rounded," it is precisely correct.

"Most of the highly creative persons we have seen are not especially well-rounded," says MacKinnon. "They have one-sided interests, and sharp edges to their personalities, and marked peaks and dips on their personality-test profiles."

This, as MacKinnon (and many others) points out, brings us face-to-face with the sharp conflict of values in our society today:

the emphasis upon the nurturing of creative talent on the one hand, and on the other "the emphasis upon togetherness, the integration of the individual into the group and its activities, good group dynamics, and smooth interpersonal relations. All our evidence points to the incompatibility of these opposed values and goals."

It is quite clear that highly creative individuals do not especially like to participate in group activities in general, and furthermore that their creative productivity is lower when they do. On the first point, to take a striking example, on a test of interpersonal behavior a nation-wide sample of creative architects revealed even less desire to be included in group activities than the personnel who volunteered to man an outpost in Antarctica during the International Geophysical Year.

On the second point — about productivity — controlled research done by Donald W. Taylor and his associates at Yale revealed that group participation when using "brainstorming" inhibits rather than facilitates creative thinking. Taylor is careful to point out that his results do not invalidate the rules of brainstorming themselves, but simply that when the same rules were used by a group and by a number of individuals working alone, whose responses were later totaled as if they were a group, the individuals working alone produced (collectively) a greater mean total number of ideas, a greater mean number of unique ideas, and ideas of higher quality. Taylor's findings have since been replicated by two other studies.

Back at the beginning of this article we said that the question of whether the truly creative person is welcome in home or classroom, business office or laboratory, could wait. It can finally be answered, of course, only by each individual parent and teacher, business executive and administrator. So far as the larger society goes, however, there is discouraging evidence that some of the dominant tendencies in American life today do not add up to the climate in which creativity flowers. These are tendencies toward conformity, toward acceptance of commonly held values and goals, toward emphasis on togetherness and the well-rounded, well-integrated individual.

But are *these* the dominant tendencies? What explains this burst of interest in creativity itself?

It is possible, of course, that creativity is now sought for spurious and superficial reasons, and that the creative person is valued simply as a potential producer of gadgets. It is possible that the whole interest is largely a fad, and that the people who are now seeking "creativity" are the same ones who a few years ago were pursuing "peace of mind" in the same shallow fashion.

It is also possible, however, that there is another reason underlying our near-obsession with the subject today. That is that the experience of this century suggests that the quality of individual life, and perhaps the survival of human life as a whole, depends on the ability and the disposition of human beings to think original thoughts, to reshuffle familiar facts into new patterns of meaning, to perceive the reality behind illusion, and to engage in daring leaps of the imagination.   ➤ VALUES FED BY THE MEDIA

If it is for this reason that we wish to nurture creativity, of both high and low degree, success in doing so is much more likely. For almost everything we know about highly creative individuals suggests that neither they nor their creativity may be used as mere means to an end, but that both will flourish when respected as ends in themselves.

C. Commentary and Analysis

Creativity, then, has entered and is firmly integrated in the productive world of big business. Nevertheless, we must remember that "creative" is the adjective traditionally applied especially to the work of artists.

Rose Slivka, editor-in-chief of the arts' magazine *Craft Horizons,* in an article on "The Object: Function, Craft, and Art" has presented some of the problems and challenges of creativity which face the contemporary artist.

First, the artist today is trying to revitalize the intrinsic value of the created object. His effort is not necessarily to create new objects. He is interested in new attitudes toward objects: in reinvesting the object with its original and intrinsic reality, value, and power.

Second, the artist is confronted with the trend toward a purely functionalist aesthetic. The creations of the new object makers face a society that has become estranged from its objects. This society no longer accepts responsibility for its objects. It is unable to see them; it uses them mechanically.

Third, contemporary man has just passed through the first generation of "expendables," plastic bags, paper tissue, ball point pens, a barrage of throwaway things, objects about which *we don't have to think*. This experience of the almost instant obsolescence of artifacts has made the artist profoundly aware of the importance of permanence and identity of materials and subject. For the artist too is aware of the possibility of his own quick obsolescence. He fears aesthetic mass production and standardized good taste.

With the approaching "new leisure" and the possibility of man exploring many creative levels of leisure, there is hope that man in his productive life and leisure will come to realize the meaning of the material object, recognize its symbolic strength, and allow matter to renew itself in power through his own human sensitivity and energies.

Creativity and Integration

The anthropologist sees in a culture *patterns* of thinking and behaving which give the community or nation its distinctive style of life, its national character. The psychologist finds in individuals and in the collectivity certain mental *patterns* which characterize the nation in its psychic, intellectual and emotional life. The sociologist finds *patterns* of social organization which give a society its distinctive individuality.

To keep a nation integrally alive and growing, all of these various patterns discovered through the social sciences must be continually reblended and recombined. The anthropolgist E. T. Hall calls this process of integrating a set of patterns into a single style "congruence." Individual men search for a personal congruity, for example, literary or scientific congruity, an *identity*. The entire culture, too, searches and strives for congruity.

It is obvious how important it is to the congruence of our culture to be able continually to integrate the world of work and leisure into the patterns of human meaning which the social scientist, philosopher and theologian each attempt to formulate. Achieving congruence on a personal and community level is a tremendous challenge to the Christian in today's world of work and leisure.

The success of this integration process — the congruity which brings about the unity and identity of a people — is largely dependent upon the creative minds in the culture. The enormous amount of creativity needed for the integration of work and leisure into the emerging structure of Christian secularity underlies the importance of studying creativity in the arts and sciences (and also in leisure, as we shall do in the following chapter) in order to obtain a true picture of the Christian and his work. Since one of the essential aspects of divinity is creativity, it is not surprising that we should expect the Christian community to be characterized by a rich creative spirit.

The creatively sensitive person usually has a highly developed sense for recognizing and working with *patterns* on one level of experience or another, for example, the intellectual, cultural, social, or aesthetic levels. He is used to making congruity out of incongruity, stretching the boundaries of patterns without breaking or destroying them. He is at home (and at play) in the areas of stress, tension and change. And in discovering new directions and approaches to the problems he faces, the creative person becomes the pacemaker; he creates new congruence, he is able to say simply and directly what the culture itself wants to say but cannot formulate.

Hence, as we said earlier, in a society where novelty and newness reign, the creative person is in great demand. In the world of work he is crucial. Without him the giant corporation would atrophy. He is essential in every sphere of life from politics to script-writing. Today creativity is a required qualification for leaders in every department of life, on the job, at home, in the community, in religious life. If a leader is not burgeoning with creativity, he had better surround himself with "idea men" or prepare to lose his position.

Knowledge and creativity are keynotes in the world of work. The two are working hand in hand to propel humanity into technological advances which children alone can calmly accept as fact. We are in an age where the incredible has become commonplace, where the unimaginable is sure to become a concrete reality in a short time. And scientists assure us (with a straight face) that we are just beginning.

Christianity today is coming to be more and more dependent upon the creative insights of its thinkers in the catechetical movement, the liturgical movement, the movement to update religious life, to mention only a few.

In the chapters of this book the focus has been placed on the world of work. The objective of these pages is to begin to formulate a contemporary understanding of the place of Christian man in the secularized world of work. One profitable way to obtain a comprehensive view of this world is to examine the meaning of work as understood by each of the various social sciences. The insights of these research workers have deepened and broadened the picture of man's interaction with the material world.

The Christian to be truly creative in reaching toward a meaning of human endeavor must discover a meaning for work which comprehends as many as possible of the results which the social scientists have uncovered for us. Only in this way will the theoretical insights regarding the meaning of the Christian at work in the world be practicable and realizable in the daily life of the Christian.

Here in the world of work more than in any other sphere of life is the most crucial challenge for the creative Christian thinker. For, if our lives are to be integrally human and Christian, this integration must occur in the Christian's daily work and his habitual attitudes toward the world of work. We are only beginning to see the deep necessity for such a Christian integration in the world of work; consequently little has been done so far by Christian theologians in this regard.

A comprehensive theology of work will have to balance and unify three points of concentration: the *future,* whose goal is called the kingdom of man, or in Teilhard's term, cosmogenesis; the *beyond,* whose goal is called the kingdom of God, or as Teilhard would say, Christogenesis; the *present,* whose goal is achieving today's task, the eight-hour day, the daily household chores. We shall return to these three focal points in the chapters on the theology of work.

It is not too difficult to develop a vision of the future or of the beyond, and there are a number of available theories to choose from if one does not feel up to constructing an original scheme. But it is no small thing to unite both goals into a Christian synthesis. Teilhard is one who has had astonishing success in this latter task with his *The Divine Milieu* and *The Phenomenon of Man*. There are however few Christian thinkers who have done serious reflection toward creating a theology of daily work. Still less have theologians tried to unify all three of these focuses of work — the future, the beyond and the present.

In emphasizing the present and the future, we do not intend to disvalue the experience of past generations. The truly creative person is keenly aware of his debt to his predecessors. To reject the past is to embrace shallowness and narrowness.

Teilhard de Chardin summarized our age in the statement that "mankind, taken as a whole, is actually in the process of undergoing, in its own way, a kind of 'crisis of puberty' " (*Cross Currents,* Fall 1952). To the degree that his insight is valid we must be careful not to be too much like the adolescent who sees the world only in the light of his limited experience, disregarding the continuity which is the history of thought and action.

In *The Christian Imagination* Justus George Lawler develops Teilhard's notion of the adolescent status of our age. Adolescence, Lawler points out, is especially a period of *self-consciousness,* both in the philosophical sense of an awakening of one's spiritual personality and also in the human sense of a deeper "realization of one's own significance in relation to other men" (p. 5).

To grow in awareness of one's personality and power to relate to and influence other men and objects is one of the richest experiences of adolescence and life itself. However, self-consciousness tends also to promote distortions, even in the interpretation of history. Hence, in the Christian community we need the creative person especially because of his appreciation of tradition and the continuity of mankind's progress toward its goal. The creative man must synthesize the past and press forward.

Questions for Discussion

1. Why is the creative person needed in society today? What basic questions did the University of California study seek to answer? What three creative types were studied? How are they distinguished?

2. What are some of the significant results of the studies of creativity? How are individuals who tend toward conformist behavior characterized when compared to those of independent behavior?

3. What new awareness does the present-day concern with creativity seem to suggest?

4. Explain some of the problems and challenges the artist is faced with in contemporary society.

5. How does creativity affect the integration process necessary in achieving new congruences? Why is this so significant for the Christian? Discuss the three time points of concentration, and the contribution of Teilhard here.

X
WORK AND
HUMAN LEISURE

A. Prenote

If the meaning of work is undergoing a metamorphosis in the
contemporary world, the meaning of leisure is in an even less
settled state. The relationship between work and leisure is not
clear. The problem of leisure is many-sided, presenting difficulties
and questions to the educationist, the sociologist, the anthropologist,
the philosopher. The Christian too faces problems when faced
with the necessity of integrating leisure into his scheme of meaning in the world of work.

Our selection in this chapter is by Fr. W. Norris Clarke, S.J.,
professor of philosophy at Fordham University. Here, Father
Clarke discusses the dimension of leisure. He shows that leisure
is a part of life soon to be more important than ever before. Integrating leisure into the life of man today demands the creativity
of all the social scientists and philosophers, artists and theologians
as well. For man must soon learn to grow and find through leisure
that human fulfillment which up to now was possible only through
work. The excerpts which follow are taken from a symposium on
The Ethical Aftermath of Automation, edited by Francis X. Quinn,
S.J. (Westminster, Md.: Newman, 1962), pp. 199-212.

B. Selection: Cultural Dimensions
of the New Leisure

All around us today, in all the main fields, there is constant
planning for the future and deliberate provoking of change for
the future.

Such planning is imperative in a world of constant and rapid change for two reasons: first, because without it you will not be able to cope with the dangers which change suddenly thrusts upon you, and secondly because you will not be able to take advantage of the constructive possibilities of the changes which do occur. It has therefore now become an essential part of the responsibilities of leaders in any field systematically to scan and prepare for the future. And I do not mean simply for next year; I mean for 10, 20, 30 years ahead.

So far, this deliberate planning seems to be going on largely on a piecemeal level — for example, the planning done by special interests, such as corporations, for their own benefit. But who is going to plan ahead for the *humanity* of man? Who is going to plan for his broad overall welfare in the next 50 years? This is certainly beyond the scope of business. Is it the work of sociology? Sociologists are indeed trying to do some of it, but it is perhaps a little too broad even for scientific sociology. Anthropologists, too, are trying their hand at it. But certainly educators, philosophers and theologians, whose interest should be in the wholeness of man, should begin to shoulder their responsibility for guiding the general movement. Otherwise, we are going to stumble blindly into the future and suddenly find ourselves face to face with some very serious human problems, too late for us to cope adequately with them.

The Fact of Leisure

In order to investigate our present problem realistically, we must start with the facts. The primary fact is that a much larger amount of leisure is in the offing for the masses of our people.

There is, it is true, still some dispute about the fact itself. Some claim that a new trend has appeared, the double job practice. Hence when the working time is cut down, workers will simply take extra jobs and have no more leisure than before. It is quite true that this practice has become at least a short-range trend in certain areas of our economy, both here and in Europe. But in view of the predominantly somber estimates put forward during this week of discussion by experts as to the slow growth of unemployment developing in the wake of automation, it seems fairly certain that in the overall, long-range picture there will have to be a progressive curtailing of the work week in order to maintain full employment in peacetime. In the face of growing unemployment, double job holding on a large scale would simply not be socially tolerated. The trend in this direction has been steady over the last hundred years, diminishing from something like an 80-hour work week in the last century to 60 and then to 40 in our own day. Now the predictions are that by the time today's children retire, or within 60 years, the work week will be down to 20 hours. And this is a conservative estimate; some claim a reduction to eight hours a week, but this seems to be more than the crystal ball will yield at present.

What we will then experience for the first time in history is a predominance of leisure over work for the majority of people. Now the first thing which we should notice about this situation is its novelty in human history. As we turn back the pages of time, it is clear that in civilized societies a large amount of leisure has always been the prerogative of the wealthy, the elite, the upper crust of society alone. Work was the lot of the masses; leisure, of the few. Now, for the first time in history, a predominance of leisure over work will become a way of life for the masses and no longer simply for the elite. This in itself is a fact of staggering implications, the more one reflects upon it.

But this is not the only element of novelty in the new situation. What we are faced with is not merely the accession of the masses to a mode of life that will still, as in the past, be enjoyed by the upper level of society. We are faced rather with a paradoxical reversal of the roles of the two groups. If present trends continue, what we shall have is actually less and less leisure for the upper strata of society and more and more leisure for the middle and lower. In order to be successful today, executives in the higher echelons, professional men, scientists, artists, statesmen, generals — in a word, the leaders of our culture — have to work 50 to 60 hours a week regularly if they wish to meet both their responsibilities and their competition. Such people simply cannot get away safely with anything like a 40-hour week. The new leisure, therefore, is really going to be the prerogative principally of the middle and lower levels of society, levels which are also, we must remember, the least educated and humanistically formed — that is to say, the least able to profit constructively from their leisure. As someone put it recently, we shall now have leisure for the masses and work for the classes.

So much for the salient facts which it seems almost certain that we shall have to reckon with. Now let us move into the area of the problems consequent upon these facts. My chief hope is to succeed in making you conscious of a radically new set of challenges soon to confront us, and to set you thinking as to what general lines of solution we must begin to plan for.

The most general problem derives from even the most casual reading of history. Wherever in the past there has been a predominance of leisure over work, it has ultimately destroyed every group that has achieved it. Abundant leisure has ordinarily led to absorption in the pursuit of personal pleasure for those possessing it. It seems to be a mysterious, fatal principle of human culture that once a group is freed of the necessity to work, the law of pursuit of personal pleasure begins to take over, becoming its dominant interest. Again and again in the pages of history, this absorption in the pursuit of personal pleasure has led, sooner or later, to degeneration — moral, intellectual, social and finally physical degeneration — and the last stage is the collapse of the society or the emergence of some new ruling class. This is the way in which the cycle runs: wealth, leisure, the pursuit of pleasure, degeneration, collapse or replacement by another group. The record so far has not been a good one for the effects of abundant leisure on those who enjoyed it. What assurance do we have that it will not work the same havoc on us?

And yet the other side of the picture is also true: There has risen an elite with abundant leisure that has frequently stimulated a flowering of the arts, letters and philosophy. Those who possessed the leisure wanted to be entertained and surrounded by beautiful things. So they sponsored artists who, in turn, contributed to the flowering of the various arts.

Among the peoples who passed through such an experience, possibly the Athenians more than any others made the most of their leisure. They were one of the few leisured elites, for example, who developed philosophers on a large scale during such a period.

One of the most significant things about the Greek concept and practice of leisure was their distinction between two kinds of leisure: the one, *serious* leisure and the other, what we might call *pastime* leisure. Serious leisure was devoted to such occupations as the theater, the arts, philosophy, politics and athletics. Pastime leisure for them consisted in relaxation, amusement, games (not the same, by the way, as serious athletics) — in a word, anything that provided rest from either work or from serious leisure. Thus we have two kinds of leisure: the one challenging, stimulating and creative; the other relaxing, distracting, restorative.

Yet it must be noted that even in Athens, the plastic artists — architects, painters and sculptors — did not come from this ruling class or elite. They belonged rather to the lower, artisan classes, because to work with the hands was considered below the dignity of the elite. Thus, even the elite of Athens did not produce from among themselves a group of creative artists.

As we ponder these lessons of history, an ominous question mark arises. Will our new leisure be a blessing or a curse? Can the masses of the future survive a predominance of leisure over work, or will the same law of history apply as it has in the past? Such questions are not mere idle speculation. The answers to them may well determine the fate of the whole form of civilization which we see developing around us today.

But since the situation itself will be unique in history, I see no necessity for assuming that the same law must inevitably work again as it has always worked in the past. I am not a partisan of the fatalistic cyclic view of history.

Active and Passive Leisure

We are now in a position to narrow down our problem. Which of the two basic ways of spending one's leisure time will predominate when the new leisure comes upon us? Will it be the unproductive pursuit of personal pleasure and amusement, the Greek pastime leisure, or perhaps more accurately, the Roman — uncreative, self-centered, self-indulgent? Or will it be spent rather in a productive, creative, serious activity that will enrich both the individual and the community?

Here, I believe, is the most crucial and fundamental question facing us. Which is going to predominate: the unproductive, rather passive pursuit of pleasure, entertainment and amusement, or productive, enriching, creative activity where the note is one of joy both in self-development as well as in a certain enrichment of the community? If the former predominates, there is no possible doubt that what lies ahead is disaster, the death sentence of our civilization. It has always been so in the past, and it is not too difficult to analyze the intrinsic reasons why it should be so on psychological and moral grounds. The basic principle involved is that where any group of people permits its energies, particularly its mental energies, to lie idle most of the time without the discipline and challenge of hard work, deterioration rapidly sets in, and sooner or later a more vigorous people, a people who are using their energies of mind and body more fully, will challenge their place in the sun and either absorb them or sweep them out of their way.

Absorption in amusement as the main occupation of one's life ends up in the inability to concentrate for very long, to discipline oneself or to stand up under a challenge which demands a long hard pull. People so occupied become incapable of anything but short-term activities to meet short-term challenges; they simply cannot cope with long-range enterprises requiring hard struggle and tenacious endurance. If our masses in the future devote the main part of their leisure time to entertainment, amusement and unproductive activity, we are certainly in for disaster, and will crumble before the rising of the African and Oriental world. A machine whose motor is kept always idling eventually becomes incapable of operating at high speeds.

Now given the inertia and weakness of human nature left to itself, it is quite possible that the masses of our people with their new leisure will tend like a dead weight to the lowest level, toward a vast bread-and-circuses kind of existence, surfeited with entertainment, bored with their gadgets, ever restlessly and purposelessly on the move at higher and higher speeds, and less and less capable of quiet reflection or of any intense, intellectual or spiritual effort. Such is one of the very real possibilities before us if we do not take thought and action now to prepare the children of today for the leisure of tomorrow.

We have sketched briefly the darkest possible alternative in our future use of the new leisure. It is time now to take a look at the brighter end of the spectrum of possibilities. This would consist in a predominantly creative, productive, personally and socially enriching utilization of their expanded leisure time by the majority, or at least by a significantly large percentage of the people. If this fork of the road is actually taken, it opens out into truly magnificent and breathtaking perspectives of a massive advance for our culture and potentially for the whole human race toward new levels of basic humanistic development and flowering of the higher faculties of man on a vast, popular scale never attained or even deemed possible before in human history. This may well be the next phase in God's long-range providential plan for the growth of humanity as a whole and of the mystical body of Christ, the Church, working as a leaven within it.

Many humanists and educators, especially those with a strong classical bent, will look on such a development as naively utopian and lacking in historical realism on the principle that high humanistic culture by its nature will always be limited to a comparatively small elite and remain out of reach of the masses. And I certainly agree with them that superior culture will always be achieved only by an elite. But higher and lower are nonetheless essentially relative terms, and the fact that the proportionate relations between the number of those on the various levels will always remain roughly the same does not by any means prevent the system as a whole from moving steadily forward and upward. May there not be laws — even humanly controllable laws — of human evolution (cultural as well as physical) just as it seems there are of evolution in the material cosmos leading up to man? Furthermore, since never before in history have the necessary conditions for the possibility of intensive humanistic development existed for the masses in any culture, the negative argument from past history can hardly be considered decisive if the time comes when these conditions for the first time become verified in fact.

Yet, to be hardheadedly realistic, in view of the endemic weakness of human nature and its proneness to yield to the forces of evil at work within it, what we shall most probably be faced with is an unstable, shifting intermingling of both the darker and the brighter possibilities, with the issue up to us (to our vision, courage, initiative, and dedicated, persevering effort, or their opposites) to swing the balance more one way than the other. One of the most crucial and indispensable steps that must be taken in the near future to tip the balance in the right direction is well thought-out education of our children for the leisure to come. And I mean education by the three great institutions equipped for it: the home, the school, and the Church.

Five Levels of Constructive Leisure

This leads us naturally to the fundamental, practical, and constructive problem with which the new leisure confronts us [and with which I shall end this paper]. What should be the general structure of a program of education for the constructive and enriching use of leisure by civilized man?

The first level, attainable by practically everybody, would seem to me to be the cultivation of some individual manual skill involving the exercise of the individual's special capacities of body, mind, and some degree of esthetic sensitivity, looked on as an expression in matter of each person's individual, human personality. It could be in do-it-yourself repairing, decorating, building around the house, in gardening, in wood or metal working, or in any other of the numberless, useful, manual arts and skills. This might well end up by restoring something like the almost vanished medieval tradition of pride in personal craftsmanship as the expression of one's personality.

Another outlet could be, and I think should be, outdoor life in its two most active and enriching forms: sports or athletics (but as an active participant, not merely a passive spectator), and vital contact with and exploration of the world of nature, especially living nature. Analogous to this, though on a higher cultural level, could be classed travel, especially to learn of other peoples and cultures or our own past. In the long run, this can gradually and unobtrusively knit the bonds of human brotherhood and solidarity more closely together (not to mention building up the visible unity of the mystical body on earth), and also consolidate more firmly man's conscious possession and domination of the globe that has been given him by God as the arena of his self-development by work and play.

The next level would be that of continued self-education through reading, education, or TV, by which everyone could make an effort to assimilate as much as he was able and willing of the accumulated wisdom and culture, scientific, literary, artistic, religious, etc., of mankind. Consider the possibilities if something like this could be made a part of our cultural ethos.

The next level would lead us into the fine arts, and by this I do not mean merely appreciation but also creative participation. Already there are some three million amateur painters in the country, and admissions to serious concerts of music have gone up 60 per cent in ten years. It is a matter of considerable dispute just how widely distributed is the ability of creative self-expression through the fine arts. There is no way of knowing for sure until the opportunity to realize their potentialities is made available to the masses. It does seem reasonably certain, however, that some significant talent along these lines is far more widely shared than has so far had the chance to manifest itself. Even though the number always remained a minority, it would not seem at all improbable that widespread opportunity and encouragement for "ordinary" people to try their hand in some way at painting, sculpture, or any one of the various fine arts, old and new, might well prove the stimulus to the greatest flowering of art in history, the principle being that the broader the base, the higher the pyramid will reach. At least the minimum that might realistically be expected is a continual movement from the higher levels of the useful arts and good craftsmanship toward the lower levels of the fine arts, if indeed it is possible to separate the two in any watertight way. Already for some years observers have noted the remarkable renaissance of interest in and teaching of art in schools and colleges around the country.

The last outlet — and we have space only to mention it — would be on the level of greater personal participation in the civic and other public life of the community, something which most people simply do not have the time to enter into at present.

This brings up the important question, which we can only call to your attention here, of whether the use of leisure should be primarily individual or primarily social. It may be that for a while at least, as long as the conditions of work tend to depersonalize the individual and submerge him as an anonymous unit in the mass, as is true for so many today, the principal function of leisure will be to restore the balance and give an opportunity for the individual initiative, self-assertion, and self-expression that has little or no outlet during the time of work. His leisure will enable a man to rediscover himself as a person. Yet we are also learning more and more that social or group activity on a truly personal basis is not a stifler but a marvelous developer and releaser of authentic, personal individuality. No one is fully an "I" save in conscious relation to some "Thou." There can be no authentic "We" save through the free, personal coming together of authentic "I's."

Secondly, start planning now how to introduce into our educational program some kind of systematic orientation of our students toward preparing for the fruitful and creative use of their future leisure. We stumbled blindly and thoughtlessly into the industrial age and are still trying to heal many of the wounds that resulted. The atomic age burst so suddenly upon us that we had no time to prepare for it and are just beginning to be aware of the magnitude of its problems. The automation revolution is being ushered in under much better control. But one of its most far-reaching aftermaths will be what some have called "the leisure revolution." If, as I together with many others believe, the new leisure will either make or break the civilization of our grandchildren or great-grandchildren, then surely we owe it both to them and to God, our common Father, to prepare in time for this new spiritual challenge to human survival and growth whose coming portents are written too clearly in the sky for us to have any excuse for not seeing them.

C. Commentary and Analysis

At the outset of our reflection we note that Father Clarke's paper did not concentrate on presenting facts and conclusions which are the result of research in the social sciences. Rather, given the problem of the leisure revolution, he chose to reflect from the standpoint of a Christian humanist upon the possibilities of leisure time.

His approach is practical in two senses. First of all, he clarifies the terms for reflection. Since the problem is one of the future, we are not dealing with past facts but with possibilities for the coming years. In light of the human socio-cultural rewards of work in a man's life which we have discussed in earlier chapters, the distinction between active and passive leisure is especially relevant in our context. Second, he classifies five levels of constructive leisure. These classes are not meant to be exhaustive or restrictive, but simply directive. The five classes are a valuable practical beginning for the Christian's reflection upon the place of leisure in his life.

From Father Clarke's discussion it is clear (1) that the leisure revolution holds in its hands the future of our civilization and (2) that we know embarrassingly little about reaping the fruits of leisure time and we have done less to find a human and Christian meaning for leisure. We must discover those dimensions of personal and interpersonal fulfillment which are attainable through the proper use of leisure.

Another near vacuum in thought concerns the Christian meaning of pleasure. There is no question that a balanced attitude toward pleasure is lacking both in our culture patterns and in the general behavioral attitudes of Christians. True, the law of pursuit of personal pleasure can lead to degeneration, especially when individuals and nations become absorbed in this pursuit. Pleasure, however, need not lead to degeneration; it can be a restorative refreshment inspiring creativity. If we are searching for a positive approach to pleasure, the words of Walter Kerr come to mind: "Pleasure is its own reward." We should approach opportunities of pleasure more openly than we have. Then perhaps there would be fewer things we may do in the name of pleasure that actually succeed in depriving us of pleasure. In "The Fine Art of Theatergoing," Mr. Kerr discusses those who approach a pleasure situation with the neutrality of a research physicist incorrectly associating the quality of indifference with pleasure.

The best way to shock oneself into a state of possible enjoyment is to know when one has not enjoyed something, and not only to know it but to confess it, to insist upon it, to shout it. Boredom should be announced; dissatisfaction should be advertised; at the risk of spoiling the party, voices should be raised. If one does not speak one's own truth, who will speak it? And if it isn't spoken, where shall its bones be laid?[1]

In the selection in chapter 3 on work and the aged the principle of the equivalence of work and play was presented. Retirement, we saw, is in many ways a passage from work to play, and the elderly individual is challenged to find fulfillment outside of the work situation. In the following chapters of reflection on the meaning of work we saw that the problem of utilizing leisure time was not merely a problem for the aging. Mankind itself is shifting from a work-centered society to an economy of abundance. This transition demands that there must be an intense educational effort to learn the arts of leisure. Such preparation must be seen as "an integral part of the educated man's training for life," says Father Clarke, "part of his responsibility to himself, to his family and to his community, to prepare himself for the fruitful use of the leisure which he will have as an adult."

The creative Christian thinker, fortified with the extra-economic meanings of work and the other values in human life, must discover how to realize for himself and his community these values and meanings more fully than ever before in leisure activities.

This reflective task of the Christian thinker upon the principle of equivalence of work and play is necessary, for it is hardly to be expected that the majority of people growing up in our present work-centered society will be able to apply in their own lives this principle of equivalence. Some psychological studies of retired workers demonstrate this incapacity of many individuals to apply the principle of equivalence. Perhaps this is in part due to the fact that many such people are not accomplished in the leisure arts. And this situation is not likely to be alleviated except through extensive education, for it is the mass of ordinary workers of the sociologically lower and middle classes who are being ushered into a mode of leisure life hitherto unknown to them. At the same time, paradoxically, says Father Clarke, trends seem to

---

[1] *New York, New York* (Delta Books, 1964), p. 44.

indicate that there will be "less and less leisure for the upper strata of society." Hence, the new leisure is really going to be "the prerogative principally of the middle and lower levels of society." Here then is the challenge of a Christian education in an age of leisure: to discover how to obtain in a revolutionary new way the fullness of human development.

In many respects one might argue that our reflections have led us from the topic of the Christian in his world of work to the topic of the Christian in his world of leisure. It should also be growing apparent that work and leisure from the viewpoint of human development are in a number of ways complementary reflections of one another, especially in the sense that some of the same human rewards (social participation, interesting experiences, opportunities for creative self-expression, sources of self-respect and the respect of others) can be obtained both through work and through leisure. This relationship between the rewards of work and leisure is logically an immediate corollary of the principle of equivalence of work and play.

The underlying philosophical truth that makes the principle of equivalence of work and play possible is that both work and play are radically human activities; both are located in the very core of the spirit of man. There are three fundamental orientations of man's work and play (leisure activity). First, man must work *and* play in the world in order to fully know and possess it; this is the orientation of scientific technology and constructive leisure. Second, man must work *and* play in the world in order to conduct, organize and integrate his actions and emotional responses toward things and people; this is the orientation of customary behavior, which includes the ethics both of responsibility and pleasure. Third, man must work *and* play in the world to most openly approach truth and love; this is the orientation of thought. And here it must be admitted that it is because man is capable of both work and play that man is capable of reflective analysis and that thought is so integral a part of all phases of human endeavor.

Work and play open the possibilities of human freedom and commitment. They make possible a dissatisfaction with the present situation and offer the potentialities to accept the challenge to change and the drive to progress.

The greatest privilege of work, says Jean Lacroix, is that it is a "mediator between nature and freedom." But this expression is true also of man's play and leisure activity. We know that work is capable of bogging man down to the point of "naturalizing" him, and also that it is capable of being a most effective factor in human liberation. We must soon come to learn that the same potentialities await discovery in man's creative use of leisure.

Questions for Discussion

1. Why is the study of the meaning of leisure relevant here?
2. What does history tell us about leisure? What are some of the elements of novelty in the present leisure situation?
3. How does Clarke outline the general structure of a program of education for leisure? What important questions does Clarke raise about the use of leisure?
4. How is the principle of the equivalance of work and play particularly significant here? What underlying philosophical truth makes this principle possible?
5. What are three fundamental orientations of man's work and play?

XI

THEOLOGY AND WORK: CREATING THE FUTURE

PART I: BASIC APPROACHES

A. Prenote I

We have surveyed the meaning of human work from the insights of the various social sciences, education, art and philosophy. In each chapter we made a short reflection and discussion from a Christian standpoint upon the material presented in the selection. The knowledge and ideas which we garnered from the data of the individual chapters gives us a foundation of information upon which to build a theology of work. In the chapter discussions certain questions about the Christian meaning of work arose which look to a theology of work for answers or at least approaches to answers. We are now ready to begin constructing the outlines of a theology of work.

We begin this chapter with a digest of an article by Fr. Joseph Thomas, a French Jesuit, who summarizes three basic approaches to a theology of work: the penitential, the creationist, and the eschatological. These three approaches form a fundamental starting point for the construction and evaluation of a contemporary theology of work. After considering the advantages and disadvantages of each view, Thomas poses some of the questions which a truly adequate theology of work must answer. The original article, entitled "Une théologie du travail?" was published in *Revue de l'action populaire* 164 (January 1963), pp. 5-18. The English digest of the article is taken from a translation by Sister Mary Nicholas, R.S.M.

B. Selection I: Three Basic Approaches to a Theology of Work

Some professional theologians have drafted the broad lines of a theology of work; among the pioneers are Fathers Chenu, Rondet, Rideau, and de Couesnongle. More than anyone before them these men recognized the urgency of constructing a theology of work. There are those who would number Teilhard de Chardin among these theologians. No one can deny Teilhard de Chardin's insights concerning the striding progress of men based on work, but Teilhard claimed only to be furnishing theologians with problems and opening dialogue with them. Some men become the voice of their times; we can at least listen to the questions they pose.

We can identify three basic views on the theology of work: the penitential, the creationist, and the eschatological.

The Penitential View

In this view, man is seen as condemned to work. An ordeal imposed as a punishment for sin, work nevertheless does carry within it the possibility of redemption. The penitential view is built upon the text of Genesis, "You will eat your bread by the sweat of your brow." This view insists on the connection between work and the struggle which man must always wage within himself. It stresses the exhausting character of the battle against a creation in revolt.

Underlying this vision is a historical situation relating to the life of the Church and the conditions of human labor. The first Christian generations were little concerned about temporal tasks and envisaged all work in the light of the imminent coming of the Lord. Furthermore, in that age the worker was considered an enslaved being. Beyond producing the necessities for subsistence, his role was reduced to furnishing cheap energy. On the other hand, by reason of the influence of Greek philosophy and the authority of a strongly hellenized wisdom literature, the Christian elite developed a general, disdainful attitude of contempt for material tasks.

Though one can challenge such a vision, this approach does have the merit of pointing out the fact that work will always be associated with toil and constraint. Without this stimulus and struggle work would become a game. The emergence of liberty in man in the midst of his natural milieu is always accomplished at the expense of the demands of nature's spontaneous whim. *with the third kind*

Spiritually, in union with Christ the redeemer man looks for the principle of a consecration of his painful efforts. Work finds a place in the growth of the body of Christ by the simple fact that growth sometimes requires painful effort. "I complete what is lacking in Christ's afflictions for the sake of his body, that is, the Church" (Col 1:24).

The narrowness of the penitential view is evident. For the teaching of Genesis cannot be reduced to a mere curse which strikes the worker. First of all, work is not the fruit of sin; it is part of the fundamental plan of God for men. When we stress only the negative aspect of work, we are not really talking about work in its fullness. Fatigue, that about work which is least truly human, is emphasized. The content of work is overlooked; the value of an effectively completed task as such does not seem to find a place in the penitential view of the plan of God.

The Creationist View

Reacting against this exaggerated pessimism, others give work a resolutely optimistic image. They rely on the text of Genesis: "Dominate the earth and bring it under submission." Thus the Christian concept of work meets the theology of the creative act.

Man is the image of God because he is a creator. God made him like himself, capable of creating and reigning over the universe and of imposing his law on it: the law of mind dominating matter. The first creation is continued; the creative action of God constantly renews itself through the action of the man at work.

Every creative effort becomes the meeting point where men come into union with God. Far from appearing as a screen between God and men, human efficiency manifests the divine efficiency which, as the true source of all creative dynamism, animates our action. In the effort of man at work, the thrust of divine love discloses itself and ceaselessly creates the world. Considered no longer in its principle, but in its accomplishments, the universe is thus that "garden" of which man is given charge. Work activates its latent energies and develops its potentialities. The balance of the world remains precarious; the adjustment of forces defines a fragile peace. From this first datum, it is necessary to construct a "cosmos," that is, to implant order and harmony there. Through work, intelligence permeates the world. In this effort man again finds the traces of the creative intelligence of God. In this sense, progress is indefinite. Only little by little can the infinite possibilities be measured. The limits of human power will never be attained nor will the resources of the universe be exhausted.

The creationist vision finds a ready audience. It establishes an authentic mystique of work: "We participate in creation." Workers find here their title of nobility: They are sons of God, formed in his image, ever more like him in the measure in which their spirit of enterprise and their boldness to do research and to accomplish things grows. Effectiveness becomes an essential duty. In an industrial civilization, it is a means of expressing charity.

In the parable of the "talents," attention is drawn to the third man condemned for his laziness and selfish prudence. Man has the duty to strive for the maximum, to seek the fullest use of all human and natural resources.

The creationist view of work is exalting but incomplete. First of all, it has little to say to those for whom work offers no element of creativity but only monotony and virtual enslavement. Second, the creationist's enthusiasm for innovation and progress cannot justify of itself the effort it entails. Without a clear goal or end for human work, any action of man would be justified in the long run, provided it were new and done with ardor. Such a viewpoint could open the way to new forms of paganism, idolatry and slavery.

The Eschatological View

A theology of work cannot be based merely on the "first creation." We are cooperators with God in building up the body of his Son. And the meaning of work has undergone a revolution; there is less emphasis upon man's discovering of the world and more upon his *project,* forming a new image of the world. Today, to dominate the earth is to dominate the future.

Thus, one cannot speak of work without considering its function in the progress of humanity toward the kingdom to come. The transformation of the universe by work would otherwise make no sense. "Must we necessarily believe that of all the works of man only his charity will perdure, only the intention which he placed upon his accomplishments?" (Rondet)

Approaches to an Integration

Many authors attempt to delineate the bond which unites theological hope, that of the kingdom of God, with the hope that animates humanity at work. There are three approaches.

First, some appeal to the necessary and mysterious maturation brought about in time. Paul speaks of the "fullness of time" wherein the first coming of Christ was realized. According to this approach, the second coming requires an analogous preparation. Doesn't the glorious manifestation of Christ suppose a certain state of the world and of civilization? Wouldn't human work have as an ultimate goal to constitute the substructure required for the final coming of the savior?

Others look beyond the horizon of history and see in work rather the preparation, direct or indirect, of the "new heaven and the new earth." Man spiritualizes this world and makes it mature for the day when creation will be ready to pass into eternity. Certain of Teilhard's formulations tend in this direction: "To mysteriously construct, first, what is capable of being divinized, then, with the grace of God supporting our efforts, to construct the divine" (*The Divine Milieu*).

The third group insists on the prophetic character of the world of man. Taken together, these works constitute a sign, a symbolic announcement of the reign of Christ and of his saints over the new universe. The kingdom of God will be ultimately established in a sudden parousia-transformation, but the progress of the universe seems already to include openings which announce that final breakthrough.

Superiority of Third View

With the eschatological view we are for the first time in a genuine Christian framework: work is situated in reference to the mystery of Christ. Human history extends its horizons to the end of time and the glorious return of the Lord. But this eschatological reflection, too new to be certain in all its terms, raises more questions than it answers.

In order to shape a theology of work the theologian faces a double task. First, he must justify (give meaning and purpose to) the present work of each individual in the light of the kingdom of God; second, he must confer a global meaning upon the work of mankind and its orientation throughout the course of history. The "end of work" is assuredly the "end of time." Still, we must not forget that in hope the end of time is both present and future, even though the end be still veiled in mystery.

The three views, purposely distinguished in a logical and abstract manner, contain elements which overlap, but they do not yet constitute a coherent exposition of a theology of work. A center of unity is missing. In giving the most important place to the mystery of the triumphant Christ, the eschatological view has the merit of indicating a path to synthesis.

What degree of immanence and "presence" does the final Christ, the pole of attraction named and recognized in faith, share with the present becoming of the world and with the labor of each man? Whatever be the level of technological development of a civilization or of an individual, what is the religious "consistency" of work and of each one's pain? Is the ultimate significance of work to be sought in the future? Finally, what link is there between the work of man and the kingdom God? We know that this kingdom is Christ both in his completion and final manifestation, and in his present growth in the mystery. "The beyond," says de Lubac, "is infinitely closer than the future." But under what conditions does the present work of each man find its place in the beyond?

PART II: GOALS OF WORK

A. Prenote II

The second selection is from a companion article to the first selection. Father Thomas here offers his own viewpoints on the Christian meaning of work and attempts to answer some of the questions raised in the earlier article. He emphasizes the eschatological approach and consequently is primarily concerned with the *future* and the long-range *goals* of human work. Christ is the center of his theology of work; the growth of the body of Christ and the sacramental source of its life are of essential importance in the work of the Christian.

The article, translated by Sister Mary Nicholas, R.S.M., was originally titled "Perspectives sur une théologie du travail," and published in *Revue de l'action populaire* 166 (March 1963), pp. 260-272.

B. Selection II: Some Views on a Theology of Work

What are the real problems human work poses for the Church and its theologians? There are two viewpoints which have to be reconciled. First, there is the question of giving meaning to the collective efforts of humanity at work, to the constant advances made by men, and to the expanding control which mankind demonstrates in its domination of the universe. From this viewpoint, theology of work concerns principally a theology of *man's accomplishments*. Second, the personal and personalist aspect must be stressed, to find the particular meaning work has for each man. Here, it is a matter of developing a theology of action, of that *human act* which is work, whatever be the age, the historical setting or technical context in which it is carried out.

In reacting against a theology and a spirituality of "pure intention," theologians have directed their thought, in a manner perhaps too exclusive, toward man's accomplishments, the results of work. The pressures of a materialistic climate and the sharpened awareness of the inhuman conditions of labor for many men have led them to the point where they identify their achievement (as "works") with the material results of their efforts, forgetting that the true achievement (as "work") lies in the labor itself. A human act cannot be considered merely a means. The act of working as such belongs to the objective order; it has duration; it contains in itself its own significance, whatever be the intentions, modes or extrinsic orientations that are brought to it. Independent of the object produced, the act of working has its own value and immanent finality by which the result, the end product, may be judged. The end product will not judge the act.

Work has an external and collective value as well as an internal and personalizing value. Each viewpoint proceeds from a different insight and demands its own method of approach.

Evolution and Meaning of Work

First of all, we should try to analyze the entire collection of phenomena related to work, to interpret the ordering of these elements, and to outline the process of evolution involved. The facts in the history of work and the skills involved in it may be easily plotted on a graph. They trace a curve indicating the constant control of man over nature. At the beginning of the graph, the curve takes a very slow rise: what does "mastery over nature" mean to primitive man? To subsist, he must first of all defend himself against nature. After its slow climb, where it would be necessary to indicate the mutual influence of technical innovations and socially acceptable ideas, the curve takes a sharp turn upward, indicating a rapid increase in the rate of expansion. Once past the critical point where technical skills joined forces with the first accumulations of capital, the curve suddenly shoots up to our era. This vertical direction of curve announces an irresistible surge forward.

From this total vision a *meaning* emerges. Our contemporaries are aware of this meaning; they are also concerned about the prolongation of this accelerated movement. The sudden acceleration of technical advancement makes it necessary to ask where we are going. Of course, beneath the reasoned movements of technological progress, historically one can discern motivation of a not-so-rational order — e.g., nations competing against one another. But too often today the dynamism of progress appears stripped of all finality; it seems to impose itself on men instead of being controlled by them. And many men who are not believers wonder about this imperative of growth and what it implies. Is all this human effort justified? No human answer will totally satisfy their doubts.

Theologians have taken an interest in this problem in the hopes of proposing for man an ultimate goal for work. While the goal lies at the end of a long process, the process itself points to, prepares for, and prefigures this goal.

The Goal of God's Plan

The real term of God's plan is the whole Christ, the perfect man, in the fullness of his stature: "to attain mature manhood, to the measure of the stature of the fullness of Christ" (Eph 4:13). Clearly, there are two complementary and distinct aspects in the unique reality of the "completed" Christ.

First of all, Christ is the completion of humanity and of creation. He "completes" them by integrating them into himself. As he is present in all men, he will gather them all in himself. Thus, in Christ is accomplished the perfect union of all mankind, a union to which all men aspire and of which the various human communities are just so many prefigurations. Since the time of the tower of Babel, hope has been directed toward this unification. One of the outcomes of history is the constantly renewed effort to establish a real communion among men within an ever-expanding community.

In still another way humanity will find its fulfillment in Christ. In the final, unquestioned submission of the universe to Christ, his life-giving power will encompass all reality. The "collective" body of each man (that world which he attempts to annex to himself) will be fully dominated and vivified at the same time as his own individual body is undergoing this process. Christ will reign over the universe, bringing to it an order, harmony and unity of which our earthly accomplishments are but faint sketches.[1]

Then will the boldest projects of men find their realization. The material world, liberated from the incoercible weight which causes it to fall back into the poorest, elemental forms of existence by the dissolution of its elements, will no longer be an obstacle for humanity, but the instrument of its total freedom. There will no longer be pain or sweat. The energy of the triumphant Christ will assure everything its final "consistency."[2] After an extended period

---

[1] St. Paul speaks frequently of this submission of the whole universe to the vivifying power of the triumphant Christ: "We await a savior, the Lord Jesus Christ, who will change our lowly body to be like his glorious body, by the power which enables him even to subject all things to himself" (Phil 3:20-21).

[2] "In him all things hold together" (Col 1:17).

in the pains of childbirth, a new world will be born, emerging from the same substance as the old world, but without the blemishes of the past.[3]

In other respects, the completion of humanity and of the universe will also be the final and total manifestation of the riches of God. Having made man to his own image and likeness, God will find in the completed Christ his perfect resemblance. The glory of God, that is, the revelation of his hidden riches and their full communication to creatures, was first dimly manifested in Adam. This glory will be found perfected in the whole Christ.[4]

The fraternal community of all men in Christ will be the perfect manifestation of the mystery of the Love which is in God and which is God himself. In this final perspective, the domination and vivification of the universe also take on meaning. Then, divine power and wisdom will be revealed and communicated in their fullness as never before.

First Drafts of the Divine Plan

The term and finality of God's plan are prefigured in the creation and history of man. Adam is the "type of the one who was to come" (Rom 5:14).

"God created man, male and female." We discern in man the traits of divine love. In the human couple we read humanity's destiny: to multiply preserving solidarity. A common origin expresses a universal fraternity which must expand without losing itself.[5] The couple is the beginning of a multiplication of fraternal relationships and is the founding principle of the human city. Created as man and woman, man discovers himself in an essential relation with the "other." Within the human city he will be drawn toward a universal communion of men through the mediation of justice and charity. By recognizing in all men another self, man opens himself to the vocation of universal love.

Moreover, God created man to dominate the earth, that is, man

---

[3] Rom 8:15-23.
[4] It is in this sense that Irenaeus wrote his famous, but often misquoted words: "Gloria Dei, vivens homo; vita autem hominis, visio Dei."
[5] Cf. the meaning of Chapter 10 of Genesis.

is capable of placing the earth at the service of all mankind. This, of course, means a domination for the good of humanity; but the plan of God also included the good of the world itself. The material world always appears as a man's "other." In this relation there is a distance to be traversed, a covenant to be established. This covenant between man and the material world is analogous to the covenant which must bring about the unity of humanity, starting from the first couple. Just as man is the creator of justice in the human city, he must also be a creator of order and harmony in the universe. Through his works, he will manifest the richness of God who shared with him some of his wisdom and power. Whatever control man may acquire over the material world finds its source in him who made man "to his own image and likeness," and in man's own creative energy.

The History of Humanity

Starting from this first principle, humanity grows and develops through the ages along two main lines.

First, humanity recognizes the growing solidarity of its members; it is always attracted by a desire for peace, the only true expression of consummation in unity. Surely, it will never achieve a definitive peace; but its history, which tends to become universal, successively engenders ever-expanding societies. The elementary forms of socialization, beginning with basic cells such as the family or the clan, are absorbed by more extensive and complex unities.

Second, man experiences in himself a determination to dominate the cosmos. It is a determination bolder and more efficacious in its results, which tend asymptotically, one could say, toward an ideal completion, namely, a perfect and permanent domination of the universe.

The main lines of this evolution are the signs of an undeniable progress. Liberty progressively emerges from a nature whose primal hostility constituted the only stimulus to liberty. It compels the blind destiny, which was subjugating it to the universe, to recede. It refuses to recognize the "elemental spirits of the world" (Gal 4:9) as the sacred and inaccessible powers upon which its fate would hinge.

Humanity assumes a solidarity with the cosmos by regarding

the domination of the cosmos as a task proposed to its freedom. Thus, humanity transforms into avoidable failings and unpardonable errors what would have been formerly considered the ineluctable workings of fate: famines, epidemics, natural catastrophes, etc. Man dares to envision a time when natural cataclysms will be ascribed to culpable negligence, to an unpardonable technical delay, or to the monstrous resurgence of collective egoism.

Is this progress? Yes. Everyone senses it. And yet, no one would be able to speak of progress without at least intimating a point of reference. The Christian, enlightened with respect to his beginning and his end, discerns in technological and economic history progress toward a "covenant" of humanity with the cosmos, a definitive alliance that is neither partial nor precarious.

This forward movement has a prophetic value. The hope of the world is the counterpart or the unconscious expression of the hope of Christ which, according to the words of Saint Bernard, is the impatience of the saints to see the completion of the body of the whole Christ. This same hope activates humanity in its effort to reach its full stature and to arrive at the completion of its own "inorganic body" (Marx). The fullness of Christ will manifest itself only after all the dormant potentialities in man have been realized. Christ will then come to "sum them up" (*récapituler*).

The global evolution of humanity at work presents signs, then, indicating the ascent toward that which will be. Do these simple signs possess their own specific objective meaning? Does the end product alone have significance? Does each step of the development derive its meaning only in reference to the future which is prefigured in it, or does it have in itself an eternal value? Technological progress discards old machines, which were at one time the objects of a pride which now seems pathetic. Is the work of men at various stages of development likewise doomed to oblivion? Is each stage merely one link in a chain where only the beginning and end matter?

In order to answer such questions, it is necessary to relinquish the collective and global point of view and consider the personal aspect of man at work. We already sense that none of the efforts and generosity of men *will be lost*. And we may go further and say that nothing *is* lost. Work makes its contribution to the growth of the body of Christ in the present moment. If our hope is to be Christian, it must turn toward the "beyond" after having allowed itself to be led toward the future.

Personal Involvement of the Worker

At whatever level it is found, all human effort cooperates in the revelation of God within man and foretells its total manifestation. All work which is truly human is the accomplishment of the mission given to Adam and the harbinger of the manifestation of the power of the Father in the glorified Christ. Each stage of the development, each act of the worker is thus the figure of the kingdom which is coming. Furthermore, each act already has its own place in the mystery of the growing kingdom, in the measure in which it is faithful to the requirements of true work.

The Act of Working

The act of working is a personal reality with structures which must first of all be defined. Like all authentic human acts, it is an involvement of the person which includes love as well as a renunciation of a certain manner of existence.

Renunciation: Like any other path to authentic liberty (a liberty which manifests itself), work is first of all the rejection of a purely natural state. In work this negativity appears to be directed uniquely toward the exterior, toward things, toward the natural state of the world. In reality, it is turned primarily and principally toward the interior, toward the natural state in which man is constantly tempted to allow himself to remain. Man works only by forcing his whole being to rise above this natural state. All work is the negation of spontaneous passivity and of instinct. Scientific reasoning, more than any other kind of reasoning, is the negator of instinctive behavior.

Work always includes a renunciation of self, whatever be its form, content or object. Its modes are varied. In work man gives his time; he "spends" his energy, he controls his most instinctive gestures and sacrifices his tendency to be capricious, passive, inattentive and irresponsible. Work cannot escape discipline and such discipline is creative. The difficulties presented by the raw materials of work are nothing compared to the interior resistance which comes from a spontaneous penchant for instinctive and routine behavior.

Modern forms of work have not eliminated these compulsions. On the contrary, if in many cases technological advances have attenuated or even eliminated physical toil, then all the more do they demand submission to the discipline of a work which becomes more collective. Besides, far from being a game, economic decisions and the power used to organize are always a risk. Under various forms, man binds himself and assumes more than ever before the responsibility of his decisions.

It is not by accident but by natural processes that through his work man is invited to "commit his life." He cannot hold on to it as a jealously defended good; however, he is offered a choice. Even though pain is inevitable, love, which gives pain its meaning, belongs in the realm of liberty. Man is always free to think that the work he accomplishes is not worth the effort he put into it; he can execute his task by submitting to it while interiorly detaching himself from it. On the other hand, he can discern in it a value which will render his efforts meaningful and justifiable; he can interiorly accept his work as a surrendering of his life out of love. Of course, this love differs from the love of gratitude expressing itself in gifts to another. Men can express as much love in their dedication to all mankind by their work as in their personal encounters in the midst of human communities.

What concrete and efficacious forms would such a love take in order to inspire work?

There would first of all be love of oneself in the noblest sense of the word. Man recognizes in his work a gateway to greater consciousness and liberty. Here, he makes himself "responsible"; he affirms his dignity, he seeks in work his self-improvement.

A love of others becomes evident. Collective work and the need for teams establish real human bonds and foster mutual help. Even in the most drastic cases of isolation, all work creates an indispensable substructure for human relations; work is communication. The most individualized work is virtually universal. Through it a dialogue is begun with everyone. Whoever works, works for everyone. The service rendered by each human being is always service for others. The whole of society is outlined on the horizon open to view; its presence is more or less well-perceived. By his work, however, man actively inserts himself into society and contributes toward building it up by his self-improvement, present and future.

This love for others is always transmitted through a love for the world. This is the specific character of work. Matter is not an enemy force to be conquered; it serves men, but men in turn serve it. At this point, work places itself at opposite poles from magic behavior. To work is to elevate things to a higher degree of perfection. Attentively, the fitter accomplishes his piece of work; the superintendent of a completed structure contemplates his construction with satisfaction. In a similar way one can sense the dawn of a true love of the world which one aspires to improve and not simply to modify or utilize. Releasing energies previously restrained, work sees itself as a creator of order and harmony, a movement toward beauty.

In the diversity of its forms, this love is nurtured by the same principle: the world is too much ours for us to treat it as something alien or indifferent. Man's efforts and nature's resources unite their respective fecundities in order to become productive. By transforming the world for greater usefulness, we become even more attached to it; we and the world have become more interdependent.

Work and Sacrifice

As for the Christian, he discovers the profound relationship between the gesture of the worker who surrenders his life through love and the mystery of Christ. Any theology of work must build upon this analogy. It underscores the traits which make human labor one of the manifestations of that "spiritual sacrifice" which humanity is called to offer. The sacrifice that was first accomplished by Christ in his individual body extends to his universal body through the intermediary of work. There are other mediations, but work is an essential one.

Accepting work and committing one's life through love mean uniting oneself to Christ's sacrifice, not by an intention that has been exteriorly imposed upon an indifferent act, but by fidelity to the profound nature of the act of working. By accepting work, one incorporates oneself into the reality of the body of Christ which grows by the extension and multiplication of his ever-present sacrifice. This is one of the dimensions of existence which is realized in the "new covenant" between Christ and man, and ultimately between Christ and the cosmos.

To work is therefore to labor for the kingdom—on condition, however, that each person truly commits himself by a free decision. But each man can just as easily shrink from his commitment in many ways. Physical laziness is nothing compared to mental laziness, especially the denial of responsibilities and capitulation to routine and comfort. How many people, even in the highest positions, see work only as a means of maintaining a certain status? How many people aspire to have a "business" but refuse to run it?

To work is to surrender one's life through love. But love can be refused. Work can be done for pure gain, but it will be done without spirit. All forms of egoism which disfigure the proper nature of work can turn one aside from the total acceptance of higher values from which work derives its meaning. Then all that remains is material work, often costly, from which the human dimension is absent. By being interiorly detached from a task that has become technical, one no longer questions himself as to the nature of his act. Besides, what one does matters little when one is no longer involved in his task.

The choice between selfishness and charity presents itself in everyone's personal life, but the social conditions of human labor, as well as its environment, influence significantly the choice that is made. Collective trends condition an individual's liberty.

Man's vocation to work is interiorly perverted by those who intend to "possess the earth" for purely personal gain instead of with the intention of controlling it in the interests of all. By denouncing the desire for personal appropriation of goods which exceed family needs, Marx is denouncing a radical perversion. The man who cares only about snatching something from the world and enjoying it, no longer loves the world. The exclusive desire to possess deforms the very act of man in his covenant with the world.

In the midst of this perverted system the Christian discovers in the image of Christ the possibility of a love which gives to work and toil a value in time and eternity. Christ extends his love of the world even to its biological and cosmic foundations. He desires its good. Of course St. Paul sees this love of Christ as giving a privileged place to his relations with the humanity he wishes to make his body and his spouse. But when Paul clarifies the meaning of the love of spouses by that universal and mysterious love of Christ for his Church, he makes use of a realistic comparison which seems to justify broadening the scope of Christ's costly and adventurous love: "For no man ever hates his own flesh, but nourishes and cherishes it, as Christ does the Church" (Eph 5:29).

Thus man loves himself through the other who becomes an integral part of himself "as his body, his own flesh." Is not this the expression of a greater love which encompasses the universe, itself destined to be incorporated into the body of Christ? The material universe is confided to man's care until the day when the covenant now inaugurated by his work will be consummated.

The Salvation of the Worker

How do the two viewpoints presented, the collective and the personal, relate to one another?

The evolution of humanity and its effort to develop find their justification in a term situated beyond history. This movement is irreversible. Before being the result of a conscious willing, this movement is a "has-to-be," a response to an unenforceable attraction. The plan for humanity seems to elude the grasp of men and project itself beyond the most ambitious objectives which men could assign to themselves. To adapt, transform, and humanize nature is still affirming very little. We dream of an alliance where nature (that "other" with which humanity is in constant dialogue) becomes ourselves. This alliance we have been striving for, and which has been attempted through centuries of fumblings and gropings, will be consummated in the kingdom. The secret desire of humanity will be fulfilled. What it tries to accomplish at the price of painful effort will be given to it. It is from the right hand of God that the perfect city will appear, to take the place of the garden entrusted to us in the beginning.

The kingdom is Christ; it is God finally recognized in his infinite sovereignty and, through the very fact of that recognition, able to diffuse the plenitude of his life throughout all of humanity. Everything will be unified because everything will have been brought under submission. The final covenant of humanity with God in Christ will seal forever all the covenants attempted here below, including the covenant of man with the world through work.

As we approach and finally reach the ultimate goal of the plan for humanity, what will remain of our attempts and gropings? Will our boldest realizations be cast aside, along with the fumblings of a faltering technology, and be forever forgotten? Of course, human accomplishments, from the first flame of fire to the man-made satellites, will not clutter up and overcrowd the universe finally reconciled to man. But the patient laborer and the expert calculator, doubtlessly surprised by the unforeseen outcome of their efforts, will not see erased in eternity the marks that work has stamped on their lives. In the struggle to overcome the hardness of stone or the pull of gravity, they assumed their vocation as men, surrendering their lives through love. Christ was sharing in the struggle as well as in the victory of these men, in proportion to their fidelity. A humble success marked paleolithic man; a more spectacular one marked the modern technician. Through their work they shared in the death and resurrection of Christ. Because in the depths of their being the kingdom was close at hand and already establishing itself, the success of their accomplishments was a sign of that kingdom.

The total domination of the universe and the perfect community of men are the unmistakable signs of the triumphant establishment of the kingdom, but they are not and will not be the kingdom itself. Heaths made to blossom or marshes dried and made fertile are not the accomplishment of the kingdom here below; but through the restoration of an endangered harmony, the kingdom present yet hidden reveals something of the passage of the risen Christ through our midst. There is no work which is not the inseparable fruit of suffering and love. There is no man at work who does not share, often without knowing it, the sufferings of Christ, his total submission, even to the point of death, as well as the triumph of the vivifying love of God in him.

The kingdom will unveil that slow becoming; it will not swallow things but it will preserve for each man the significant traits of his personal adventure. This is what the affirmation "the body of man will rise" signifies and implies.

Would charity, in becoming universal, break the bond of a personal relationship formed here on earth between two beings? Will not the particularity of conjugal love be eternally assumed in the form of a preference? Why then could not the elementary cells of human relationships that history has expanded little by little at the center of more vast groupings of people keep their specific value in a community enlarged to the dimensions of a total humanity, so that individuals would be able to recognize themselves as members of a particular group?

The same thing applies to the awkward human beginnings eclipsed by the soaring speed of technical growth. Today the humble first-fruits of human effort are rejected, forgotten, scorned. Just as men once loved the harsh, unfriendly environment which would not spare them, why could not the men of today, marked by great efforts, bring a proper way of loving to the world?

We talk about progress where it would be more fitting to discuss diversity. Today the goal of our ambitions is more easily discerned, but this goal was already there, stamped upon the stumblings of primitive humanity. It will be accomplished for everyone. The new world which will be offered to them will not only be in the measure of their dreams; it will be even more than that. It will be in proportion to their fidelity.

Work and the Eucharist

At this point it is not difficult to perceive the special bond that links work with the eucharist, "this sacrament of the spiritual sacrifice of humanity" (St. Augustine). Theology can deepen this association along two lines.

First of all, the eucharist is sacrifice. Christ delivers up his physical life, refusing to "jealously cling to it" (Phil 2:6). He makes of it a "thing" left to the disposition of God, of men, and of all who would receive it. Doesn't the worker, too, expose his life to the mercy of the forces of nature he must challenge? He abandons his life to the mercy of others whom he must consent to serve, whatever his station in life — whether he is more or less independent, whether he is of higher or lower status. In work, the humanization of nature has as a counterpart man's "naturalization." But the naturalization process goes further than Marx believed. For a part of the self goes out to become "nature," to become a thing. Even if there is no alienation, work is and will always remain objectification. Before it is a means of self-assertion, work will always be a consent to giving, a going out of oneself.

Second, the theology of work will perhaps permit us to explore an essential dimension of the eucharistic mystery quite neglected in our day. The questions of transubstantiation and the real presence are, of course, no longer as hotly debated as they were in the sixteenth century, but it seems these topics have been quite overshadowed in favor of speculation on the sacrificial aspect of the act of consecration itself. The present tendency could hardly lead to a theological development of the meaning of the host changed into the body of Christ, the very place where we find the ultimate meaning of work.

Here indeed, at the consecration, is realized the change from material substance into the body of Christ himself. The very term of all human work is present under the appearances of bread and wine. The material world and humanity are reconciled in Jesus Christ. Matter is not only humanized, it is spiritualized and divinized. The host is in different, yet real ways the figure of the material world in its ultimate state and the figure of humanity in the completion of its unity.[6] Finally, Christ himself is there, as at the end of time he will manifest himself as universal Lord and Savior. And the host reveals to us that this completion is already realized at the present time here below. It is the first sign, which discloses that everything else is nothing but sign. Over and above the appearances, the eucharist nourishes our faith and our hope in a reality which we can perceive, and in this atmosphere we make our way along the road.

Perhaps that would have been the merit of Teilhard, to call attention back to that "substantial" aspect of the eucharistic mystery. The consecration of the host points out the meaning of the consecration of the world and of humanity which seeks to share this solidarity through its work. In the host we receive "the bread of our work, the blood of our effort."

The theology of work is not lacking in avenues to explore. How-

---

[6] Cf. "Vos estis quod accepistis" (Augustine): "It is yourselves whom you have received."

ever, it must avoid developing merely for its own sake. It must avoid restricting its object to human work only, otherwise it would risk reaching an impasse.

From a purely theological viewpoint, reflection on work leads to posing in a more synthetic manner certain problems about creation which are often approached in a haphazard way. With regard to creation, final ends, the Church, and the eucharist, theological reflection will recall certain classical theological categories and at the same time will be an incentive to their renewal. If the relations of the "natural" and of the "supernatural" have instigated passionate debates, it is no longer sufficient today to wonder about the natural or supernatural destination of the spiritual creature. The question is posed in terms of liberty and history. How is the coming of the kingdom of Christ in history brought about? We hope for the kingdom, certainly as a free gift, and at the same time we collaborate in its coming. What connection is there between theological hope and human hope and the projects which are animated by human hope? [7]

On the other hand, any consideration of work has to be resituated in a global vision of history and of human society. Work only builds the city of man when it is subject to the city of man. It is the human city which gives work its orientation and bestows upon work a meaning. Only in this perspective does work become human.

Work is nothing without communication. The man at work is a person who is especially summoned to answer to words which make him a responsible person. There alone can the two views of global expansion and the "drama" of personal existence be related. Perhaps introducing the dimension of the Word at the very heart of technological activity will allow an authentic theology of work.

---

[7] What should be retained, for example, of certain texts of St. Paul: "For the creation waits with eager longing for the revealing of the sons of God; for the creation was subjected to futility, not of its own will but by the will of him who subjected it in hope; because the creation itself will be set free from its bondage to decay and obtain the glorious liberty of the children of God. We know that the whole creation has been groaning in travail together until now; and not only the creation, but we ourselves, who have the first fruits of the Spirit, groan inwardly as we wait for adoption as sons, the redemption of our bodies" (Rom 8:19-23).

Work and Word, technology and politics, are inseparable. Both will find a place in a theology of the Church, where the mystery of history and of the kingdom converge.

C. Commentary and Analysis: Parts I and II

Work has an external and collective meaning as well as an internal and personalizing one. From this radical insight Thomas generates some valuable conclusions.

First, in reflection on the external and collective value of work he finds in the drive toward the *future* the symbol and prefiguration of the *beyond*. He sees this interrelation between the kingdom of God and the kingdom of man existing on the level of the fraternal community as well as on the level of technological achievement. For "the plan for humanity seems to elude the grasp of man and project itself beyond the most ambitious objectives which men could assign to themselves."

Second, Thomas emphasizes the symbolic value of the *present* in creating the future: "In the human couple we read humanity's destiny: to multiply preserving solidarity." Similarly, "man experiences in himself a determination to dominate the cosmos." And from the same viewpoint "humanity assumes a solidarity with the cosmos by regarding the domination of the cosmos as a task proposed to its freedom." Thomas also speaks of the forward movement of mankind as having a "prophetic value." Hence, we might say that Thomas' major emphasis is placed on *Christian hope,* that is, on the global evolution of humanity as a sign of what will be.

Note that even Thomas' concern with the work of the *individual* is focused upon the future. For example, he asks whether or not the work of a man is doomed to oblivion when his achievements are superseded. Will the worker's efforts or generosity be lost? He assures us that each act of the worker "already has its own place in the mystery of the growing kingdom."

Third, in his discussion Thomas characterizes the act of working as "love for others . . . transmitted through a love for the world." This love is fostered by the principle: "The world is too much ours for us to treat it as alien or indifferent." This love of the world wants a fuller development and discussion and will be met with in the next chapter.

One of the most significantly Christian insights which Thomas presents in the light of the principle "the world is too much ours . . ." is the difference between approaching work through selfishness and through charity. Each man has a choice of "possessing the earth" for purely personal gain or "with the intention of controlling it in the interest of all." Through Christ the Christian discovers the possibility of a love which gives to work and toil a value in time and eternity.

Fourth, Thomas shows how work is the seed and fruit of suffering and love, and thus work becomes a vehicle for our following of Christ. He also shows the bond between work and the sacramental life of the Church; work possesses the eucharistic aspects of consecration, transubstantiation, and real presence.

Finally, we should not hastily pass over further theological questions which work poses "in a more synthetic manner," for example, regarding creation, final ends, the Church and the eucharist; the connection between theological hope and human hope; the place of communication within the city of man as well as in the eschatological community. These and other related questions spawned by Thomas' theological reflection on man in his world of work cry for solutions. The fact that they receive little mention and discussion in these pages should in no sense lead the reader to consider them unimportant.

Perhaps the weakest aspect of Thomas' treatment of the meaning of work is his lack of emphasis upon the *present*. His inspirational visions of the *future* and the relation of the future to the beyond are well developed. However, in this context the present tends to be read merely as a symbol or sign of the future and the beyond. But the present is far more than this. In the purely symbolic context, the importance and potential of the present *for itself* as well as the fullness of man's intimate relationship with the created world receives inadequate emphasis.

From the direction of this anthology, the reflections we have made upon the selections in the earlier chapters indicated that there is a deep need for understanding work in today's context if we wish to realize an integrated meaning of all human activity, both personal and productive. Consequently we focus in the following chapter on the Christian meaning of the present, upon living and working in the created world.

Questions for Discussion

1. Describe each of the three basic theological views of work summarized by Thomas in Part I of the chapter.
2. Which does Thomas think supplies a truly Christian framework? Why?
3. How does Thomas relate the collective accomplishments of mankind with the work of each individual in Part II? Consider here his treatment of evolution, fulfillment in Christ, Adam, human history, love and renunciation, work and sacrifice.
4. What are the main lines of Thomas' development of work in the context of the kingdom of Christ and of the eucharist?
5. In what ways are Thomas' views related more to the future and the beyond, and less to the present? Discuss.

XII
THEOLOGY AND WORK:
CREATING THE PRESENT

A. Prenote

The intent of this chapter on creating the present is simply to balance Thomas' (and others') emphasis on the future and the eschatological term of the work of mankind. The final essay concentrates on work as a daily, here-and-now experience, as a confrontation of human effort with material reality, emphasizing the nondivine on both sides of the confrontation. The theology of work cannot avoid a study of the world *as world* and the possible attitudes Christians may take as they encounter the secularized world precisely in its materiality.

Many contemporary Catholic as well as Protestant theologians are involved with such problems as the meaning of the created world in the divine plan. *The Christian and the World* (New York: Kenedy, 1965), volume 3 of the Canisianum readings in theology and *The Church and the World,* volume 6 of the Concilium series (Glen Rock, N.J.: Paulist, 1965) are two excellent collections of essays connected with problems brought about by the advent of secular Christianity.

The selection "Toward a Theological Meaning for the Daily Work of Christians" is an essay written by the editor, Louis M. Savary, S.J. It draws its inspiration, ideas and content from two sources: Christopher F. Mooney's *Teilhard de Chardin and the Mystery of Christ* (New York: Harper, 1966), and Johannes B. Metz's "A Believer's Look at the World: A Christian Standpoint in the Secularized World of Today," in the collection mentioned above, *The Christian and the World: Readings in Theology,* pp. 68-100.

B. Selection: Toward a Theological Meaning
for the Daily Work of Christians

For the Christian, encounter with the world always presupposes encounter with Christ and with his Church. The Christian who wishes to confront the world and express himself productively therein must first encounter Christ in the personal self-expression and receptivity of love. The Christian must at the same time accept in faith the invitation to commit himself to the community of persons fused in love which is the Church. In this atmosphere of the grace of Christ and the fellowship of his body the Christian is prepared, but not fully, to encounter the world and transform it. There is also the life of human wisdom in which the Christian must be at home and to which he must be committed. For in any realm of living, commitment is a necessary condition for greatness.

Before we can dare to begin to live for God we must begin boldly *to live;* before we can presume to think about God we should previously have been courageous enough *to think.* Faith emerges not from refusing to think but from the persistently eager search for truth wherever it can be found. Experiencing weakness and darkness in the depths of human knowledge is what beckons us to step forward with courage into the unknowns of the realm of faith, convinced that God wants this exploration and reaching and will remain at our sides as we seek. It is grace which healthfully infects human inquisitiveness, grace which will not let us sit back drowsily as if all matters were already settled and in full maturity. For it is faith that makes us feel the dull pain of monotony and dissatisfaction, hope which creates in us the need for continual rejuvenation and experimentation, love which makes us plunge into the mystery of the created world, invited there by God.

The Christian Tension in Work

And yet, in confronting the world there is a tension which the Christian feels. Teilhard de Chardin expressed it thus:

> How can the man who believes in heaven and the cross continue to believe seriously in the value of worldly occupations? How can the believer, in the name of everything that is most Christian in him, carry out his duty as a man to the fullest extent and as wholeheartedly and as freely as if he were on the direct road to God? That is what is not altogether clear at first sight; and in fact disturbs more minds than one thinks (*The Divine Milieu,* p. 19).

Teilhard brought the problem of work into a fundamental clarity and made great strides into a meaningful way of approaching the mystery. It is clear from his letters, moreover, that this intellectual and theoretical problem reflected a psychological conflict for Teilhard as well. In his own religious spirituality he tried to bring into a single concrete focus both his attraction for matter and his adoration for the person of Christ. This search for the meaning of human effort and his love for the earth were responsible for his interior struggles and his progress in the spiritual life. Later in life Teilhard admitted that "whatever we do in this regard, we are not going to arrive at any perfect reconciliation between God and the world. Christ will always be the 'sign of contradiction.' " Can the Christian foster a passionate and legitimate love for the earth and human progress and unite it with a unique pursuit of the kingdom of heaven? This is the dilemma which Teilhard and many with him feel poignantly. Such men cannot deny the irresistible attractiveness of all the currents of the cosmos which men instinctively love and which constitute life as a human being.

Two Questions and Two Facts

This dilemma brings into clear focus two fundamental questions facing the Christian who confronts the world in human effort.

First, man himself is certainly the most important creature in God's universe; but what of material being, matter itself, what is the purpose of the earth and its potentialities, what is its meaning in God's plan? Is it a mirror that man polishes in order to see God's face, or his own? Was it perhaps created as a toy to delight man, to be thrown away when man puts away the things of child-hood?

Second, the Christian must discover what acts of man actually help to build the kingdom of God. This is important, for unless the Christian, who is trying to live in the kingdom of man as well as in the kingdom of God, has some guideposts to identify the nature and quality of his efforts in the world or some indication of how he is affecting the kingdom of God, he is no surer of the value and meaning of his work than any other man. For if the two kingdoms are practically indistinguishable, does it make any difference be-haviorally whether a worker is Christian or not, especially since human progress seems to depend simply upon human skill and effort?

Any attempt to answer these two fundamental questions must take into account two facts.

The first fact concerns the paradox men observe between man-kind's global progress on the one hand and the failure and regres-sion of individual men and nations on the other. In the words of Father Mooney:

> Christian assurance of humanity's ultimate return to God be-comes much less serene when faced with the drama and tragedy of human life, the sinfulness of man, his need of mercy and forgiveness, the mystery of the cross and the passion, and that mysterious power of Satan to pervert the good that men do (p. 205).

Immediate experience is filled more with tension than with security, more with hesitation than confidence, more with trial and error than with continuous advancement, more with the kingdom of man than with the kingdom of God. Faith tells us of God's total plan for the human race but the concrete future remains unknown to man.

The second fact that must be considered is secularization and the powerful influence it has made and continues to make upon the Christian as he lives in the world and works with materials and men. For whole classes of men work has come to have little human meaning and no longer any religious value. The impact of secularization upon Christianity is reflected in the enormous output of theological literature on the secular interpretation of the gospel. As we watch the secularized world coming to accept the responsibility for the common needs of mankind — discovering, ordering and integrating human values — we also see the Church in its theologians re-evaluating the Church's relation to the world.

Approaches to the Problem

Any attempt to answer the problem of human work and the Christian's relation to the world must take into consideration the two facts presented in the preceding paragraphs: the tension between progress and regression, and the universal influence of secularization.

For this reason, in our contemporary context it is harmful and useless to attempt to restore the religious significance of work and its integrity in human life by simply advising the use of external moral remedies, to make work merely the object of a pure intention.

On the other hand, it is wrong to deify work as some do, to turn it into an act of worship. For in the end this leads to a denial of God and fails to satisfy man's need to worship. In our age of secularisim man sees human activity as *human* activity, the material world as *material* world. He experiences his work as *human* effort confronting the *material* world. Of this we are certain. Hence, any Christian approach to the world or to work must acknowledge this fact. Work is seldom experienced as a supernatural act.

A third attempt at a solution to the problem of work asks the Christian to insert the secular world of today into what G. Thils calls "a theology of earthly realities," into that immanent immediacy of God where man is able somehow to *see* himself immersed in a divine atmosphere. Secularization, however, has forced us to admit that we, unlike medieval man, cannot actually perceive such a divine atmosphere. Whatever awareness we have of such an immersion into God's life is by logical implication from faith, which, though true, is nonetheless imperceptible in daily experience.

A fourth approach is to inculcate in the Christian an unprejudiced "openness to the world" with the clear goal of *assimilating,* like food, this secular world and giving it a new foundation in the mystery of Christ. In this conception, the world and its potentialities appear as the *immediate material* of Christian activity. That the secular world possesses a new foundation, new roots, in the mystery of Christ is certainly true. It is furthermore essential to affirm that mankind and the created world draw ultimate meaning and finality only in relation to Christ and through Christ to the Father. However, this assimilating-the-world approach bypasses a very fundamental theological implication which is recognized and reaffirmed by secularization: that humanity and the created world possess an identity distinct from God with a certain autonomy and mediate finality which is intrinsic.

Secularization as a Positive Christian Value

We may legitimately ask, then, if secularization has removed the possibility of a Christian starting point or meaning for human effort. Does Christianity still remain effective in this historically growing secularization? How is the Spirit still poured out upon the face of this secular world? In the article on "A Believer's Look at the World," Johannes B. Metz argues that the theologian must see in the process of secularization a *positive* Christian value. If secularization is not merely an event in world-history but also one in salvation-history, "the secularization of the world is not unambiguously the world's protesting rejection of God's acceptance of it, but is also primarily the historical manifestation of its acceptance by God" (p. 71). Metz believes that secularization as it confronts us has come about in its broad lines "not in spite of *but on account of Christianity.*" Secularization in its origin is a Christian event. God took the world to himself definitively and finally in Christ (2 Cor 1:19f.); the Church is the historic, visible and effective sign and sacrament of the eschatologically definitive acceptance of the redeemed world by God.

The world which God has accepted and acts upon is not only nature but essentially the world of man and history, hence necessarily a world marked by man's understanding and free choice, by man's creative personal and productive self-expression. The world must seek to nourish the seeds which have been planted in it. "It must seek its own reality," says Metz, "in order to become that which through Jesus Christ it already is: the new age, the 'new heaven and new earth' (Apoc 21:1), the single kingdom of God and man" (p. 74).

How God Relates to Creation

What God takes to himself he does not violate or destroy or absorb into himself in the bad sense of pantheism. Rather God allows the other to remain distinct from himself; he admits that the other has its own properties and characteristics and independence: "He can and wants to accept the other precisely in the respect in which it differs from himself, in which it is not divine but rather human and worldly" (p. 76). By his acceptance of the world he sets it free (cf. John 8:32) for its own authentic mode of being. God does not rival the world, he increases its importance. Only when the world has been accepted by God does it become itself in all its deepest worldly potentialities, and this is precisely because it is thereby taken into the trinitarian life of God.

The relationship between God and the created world is analogous to a friendship between two human beings. In friendship two persons give themselves to one another. In this mutual exchange, in belonging to the other, individuality is not destroyed but rather blossoms in its true uniqueness. In a similar manner, God's liberating acceptance of the world enables it to belong to him in the deepest sense without in any way losing its own identity. Thus, when God approaches the world, the distance and differences between God and the world do not disappear but, paradoxically, only then at last become clearly visible. The world then appears fully as worldly and God fully as divine. It is the world "precisely in its nondivinity or its worldliness" which God claims for himself.

In recognizing this fundamental relationship, the Christian will avoid a certain shallow incarnationalism "which allows the world to be divinized directly through the incarnation or which interprets salvation history itself as the growing divinization of man" (Metz, p. 78). Such a shallow theology would ultimately eradicate a need for *creative* man, would render absurd the drives man has to control the earth, to lose himself in the attraction of matter; and the world would be a place where the finite "yes" of man in response to the gift of the universe would be a mockery, for man's work would be useless and what he thinks is his free will is in reality nothing at all. From man's viewpoint, in such a theological setting nature would then become one huge divine April fool's joke.

In the theological context presented by Metz, the Christian is expected to be an image and likeness of God and to act accordingly. For he must, like God, allow the world to be wholly worldly. This is the goal of his work; not to divinize the world but to remove the aura of divinity from it. Metz feels that behind the process of secularization there lies a genuinely Christian impulse.

This process in its basic trait (admittedly *only* in this) is directed not against a Christian world-view, but rather against an immediate cosmic divinism. Indeed, this process appears to represent exactly what has occurred in our world situation through the Christ-event (p. 81).

The Christian's task, therefore, is to accept the world as world and set it free. This is the challenge to his creative love and work. The process of secularization will never be wholly under his control and never wholly comprehensible to him.

The Importance of Christ

At this point Metz makes a special effort to point out the following:

. . . we ourselves can never assimilate the world in such a way that its secularism appears as the *pure* expression of our acceptance, of its liberation through our faith. For the origin of this liberating acceptance of the world is not in ourselves. Its origin is nothing other than the *descensus* of the Son, in whom the Father has definitively taken the world to himself. Because we do not accomplish this acceptance, but only re-enact it in the grace of Christ, the secularism of the world never appears to us as receiving its equilibrium and its freedom from our acceptance of it in faith (p. 89, note).

Consequently, secularism always appears as something beyond

our control, something we cannot describe or comprehend. In this sense secularism is really pagan and profane; we shall always have to suffer from it and bear it as the cross of our faith. In this sense Paul is crucified to the world and the world to him (Gal 6:14), not in spite of his acceptance of its secularism but precisely *because* he accepts it in faith and because it is for him something painfully strange and estranging in the center of his life and faith. God alone in the incomprehensible mystery of his love is the only locus of genuine interpenetration between faith and the world.

What this means for the Christian and his work is that his faith in Christ and basically his faith alone can boldly stand up to the worldliness of the world and take it to himself as it is. Only on the strength of God's liberating acceptance of the world can man confront the world without giving his allegiance to new gods. Metz feels that this need of faith is so essential that one is compelled to say that whenever a non-Christian sincerely confronts this worldliness of the world, he does it by virtue of a hidden Christianity. Otherwise the deep secularity of today will lead the nonbeliever to believe in false ideologies, a utopian progress, or nihilism or skepticism. The non-Christian must base his life on myth; only the Christian is the truly "worldly" man, "for only he can tolerate what is truly worldly," since in faith he re-enacts that act which gives everything worldly in the world its being and its life: God's liberating acceptance of the world in Christ.

Through his faith the Christian is forced to be active; he cannot remain passive or indifferent to the world. The human work of Christians is thus the highest completion of the world in the spirit and power of that freedom and love into which we have been introduced by Christ. The Christian's task is to intensify worldly reality, to discover by his effort those deeper dimensions which the material world concretely contains but which it cannot realize by itself. Because of God's saving intervention in history, the Christian vision opens to man's creative effort the possibility and to some degree of obligation

> . . . to make the world more worldly, to bring it into its own,
> to preserve the barely suggested, barely dreamed-of heights
> and depths of its own worldly nature which have been made

possible by grace, but have been hidden and obstructed by sin (Metz, p. 93).

Conclusion

The foregoing reflections are not proposed in any way as a total Christian spirituality. The emphasis in this essay was upon man's daily confrontation with the world in work and the meaning of this Christian encounter from a theological point of view in today's secularized world.

We sought, in particular, the beginnings of an approach to a theology of work that could be of personal value to the Christian toiling behind a machine in an automated factory as well as to the research scientist standing on the frontier of human knowledge. As a modest beginning, we attempted to apply Metz's insights to some of the problems of work, especially as they occur in the daily worklife of the Christian.

There appear to be at least four advantages in employing this theological approach which finds a positive Christian value in the process of secularization:

(1) *The Christian can face the world as world.* He is not asked somehow to discover Christ latent in the earth or somewhere within the materials of his work.

(2) *The Christian can face the material world as material world in his concrete daily activity.* He is not expected to divinize it or purify it or in some way to stamp it with a supernatural seal, but simply to acknowledge the meaning and mediate finality which it possesses in itself. This he does without ever denying that this creation with which and in which he works has ultimate meaning and finality only in relation to the Creator. Furthermore, the Christian in his work remains free to follow his own natural inclination and vision under the direction of the Spirit of Christ and to attempt to bring his vision ever closer to fulfillment.

(3) *The Christian can face the present as present.* There are some favored men who possess and are possessed by a vision of human progress and who burn with desire for its completion in Christ and who are able to work with their eyes on the *future*. For the Christian who lacks the ability to grasp the meaning of his work in terms of God's total plan in a vision of the future, the

present approach offers him the possibility of learning to find an immediate meaning in his effort to express more clearly as world the world of today.

(4) *The Christian may perform his human activity as human activity.* He is not expected to experience the supernatural efficacy of each of his human actions, yet he is assured that whatever work he does to clarify and build the kingdom of man is also helping to clarify and "distinguish" the kingdom of God.

Hopefully, with the fresh opening provided by Metz's insight and its future theological development, Christians may be able to encounter the world in work more authentically both as sons of men and sons of God.

C. Additional Observations

Once again we remind the reader that this essay on the daily work of Christians is not intended to present anything but a single aspect of a many-sided problem.

It will be profitable at this point to present in very summary fashion a discussion of the three most important focuses of a theology of work as implied in our survey of the meanings of work through the social sciences, education, art, philosophy and theology: the future, the beyond and the present.

For in the final analysis, the most important implication for the Christian and his work in today's world is the following: *If human effort is to possess an effective significance in the Christian's life and community, his work must be integrally viewed in relation to the future, the beyond and the present.*

The Future

In man's fascination with time and its meaning, no one can deny the special allure of the future. The past is seen as accomplished fact, while the future appears as material for man's molding of hands and mind.

In *Building the Earth* Teilhard de Chardin claims that there are three major influences confronting each other in the world today and struggling for possession of the earth; he calls them democracy, communism, and authoritarian nationalism (or fascism). Each of these three ideologies, characteristically, places great trust in the future. Each of them has its own passionate aspiration; each of them, says Teilhard, is misunderstood or imperfectly comprehended. Democracy's *passion for the individual* rather than freeing man has merely emancipated him; communism's *passion for the universal* is determined to exploit the total potentiality of matter and has forgotten the spirit; fascism's passion for the future focuses upon the *ideal of an organized elite*. None of the three existing movements is totally satisfactory. Each however holds some positive value for civilization. It is man's responsibility to discover and unify these values. Teilhard feels that "the three currents will find themselves merging in the conception of a common task; namely, to promote the spiritual future of the world . . . all the world is finally at one in recognizing that the function of man is to build and direct the whole of the earth" (p. 35).

No theology of work can avoid the future, the goals of human effort. Any human activity becomes depressing drudgery when it is seen as humanly meaningless. When, however, man is given a river to bridge, a planet to reach, a blueprint to bring into reality, his powers of enthusiasm, energy, responsibility and commitment are called into being. Witness the technological goals and movements in recent history which have given birth to undreamed-of effort and ingenuity.

In fact, no nation can survive without a purpose or a goal. Today the world itself seems to demand its own purpose and goal for its survival. For the Christian, the depth of insight and generosity that is needed to comprehend the complexity of such a goal and integrate it into the setting of faith is overwhelming.

The solution to the fundamental tension between this world and the next lies in the future, says Teilhard. He believed firmly that the future hides a point where the cosmic and Christic movements inevitably converge.

The man who is possessed with such a vision of human progress and its completion in Christ is a favored man, indeed. Such a man feels it a sacred task to advance life on earth. His effort in this regard, springing from faith and a right intention, Teilhard tells us, will constitute one of the most practical and effective factors in this man's sanctity.

The Beyond

Concern for the future is basically a concern for the kingdom of man; concern with the beyond is basically a concern for the kingdom of God. Although the natural and anthropological sciences show us that matter is directed to and toward the spirit, these disciplines can tell us nothing about the parousia-transformation which is to occur at the second coming of Christ. Though we know very little concerning this eschatological event, theologians assure us that the Christian is justified in seeing some sort of "continuity" in which this earth, just as the Christian's own body, will be transformed in that great instant.

However little the Christian knows about the nature and manner of the birth of the New Jerusalem on the last day, he must nevertheless maintain an eschatological perspective in his life and work. For the materials with which he works, his fellowmen and his own life and power are all gifts of God and will take part in the consummation of the world. Furthermore, whenever the Christian acts, he acts fundamentally in union with Christ through faith, striving to attain the kingdom of God in the totality of his actions.

Hence, an understanding of the place of Jesus Christ and the Church in the mystery of creation is very essential for the Christian and his work. In his book on *Justification* (New York: Nelson, 1964) Hans Küng shows how God's plan of salvation was already operative in creation, how the mystery of the Church was hidden in creation, how in creation God conceived the plan in Christ for the salvation of all men through the Church (p. 137).

Küng reminds us that we must distinguish a double gift from God: creation and creation in Christ. "Otherwise the specifically supernatural character of the order created in Christ would not be guaranteed" (p. 144). This double gift founds the two kingdoms, of man and God, and leads us at once toward the future and the beyond.

Behaviorally speaking, however, it seems in the experience of many men that in any particular human event it is practically impossible to distinguish the kingdom of man from the kingdom of God. For God's gratuitous interventions are so continual and so inseparably united to natural human activity that one can never know concretely to what degree any given action is supernaturally salvific. It seems that in this regard the Christian must be satisfied with a more generalized attitude of openness to God and an awareness of the supernatural horizon of his acts through faith. For some men the awareness through faith that grace is an encompassing medium of their lives allows them to taste the experience, in Karl Rahner's words, "of an infinite desire, of a radical optimism, of an unquenchable discontent."

The Present

The principal concern of this book has been with the present, with the meaning of work for the Christian today, in this world. In the past daily work never seemed to pose much of a problem for the Christian, since for the most part he was simply forced to work in order to buy bread to live. He was told that he would please God by doing his job faithfully and well and "offering" it to God as some kind of act of worship. And he was taught to believe that by doing this everything would turn out profitably for himself and the kingdom of God.

There really was no sufficient reason offered for working faithfully and well, except that work was *owed* to the employer in return for wages. In this context it made little difference whether a man's occupation was dusting corridors, performing heart surgery or flying a commercial airliner, provided he belonged to the faith and at least from time to time affixed an "intention" to his activities. The theological shallowness of this approach has been recognized as well as the harm done in the devaluation of various human efforts and skills which this approach encouraged.

With the new theology of the world being developed among Christian thinkers, we are discovering a much richer and more solid foundation upon which to build a theology of work. With this theological basis and with the emphasis placed upon recognizing the importance of the present, the material, the nondivine, and the world — recognizing them for what they are — today's work will not only be looked at in the light of the future and the beyond but will be able to be seen in the light of the present more clearly than ever before. This approach which emphasizes the present (and which is only beginning to be applied in various areas of Christian life) neither denies nor distorts the future or the beyond but brings them into clear perspective. The man who has his visions of cosmogenesis and his hope in Christogenesis will find them in this light more sharply defined, more brilliant and beckoning. And the man who cannot see the *end* of the road or who desires it only minimally, at least can come to understand and find meaning in his own way, however confused, in making the world recognized as world.

In either case the Christian is responding to the world which cries for its own existence to be recognized and related to. He does not apply indiscriminately to human and earthly pursuits the eternal values of which he knows himself to be the bearer. He recognizes the essential dimension of man, says Chenu, "who cannot attain eternity except through living in time, and who, in reality, can only become master of himself by identification, as a member of the community, with the dynamic of history" (p. 47).

The Christian and the Church

It is one thing to be captivated by the future, by the world visions of men like Teilhard de Chardin, and quite another thing to realize such a vision, even in a small way, within one's own daily activities. Moreover, it is not very easy to see a day's work at the typewriter or the drill press in terms of the beyond, as part of the march of Christian mankind toward the new Jerusalem. In fact, it is difficult to see how our commitment to Christianity and our world vision are having any effect in the city of man today. For the present status of Christianity as a religion is a lowly one in our secularized world. Christian values are not dominant in our country. In time of crisis the decisions will be made by men whose values are basically non-Christian. "At work, in leisure, in political, social, sexual, educational, professional and family life," said Cardinal Cushing, "the mass of the modern community is almost without trace of Christian values." In the face of these facts we hear the words of Pope Paul VI enunciate the deceptively simple and sublime objective of the Church:

> The mission of the Church today is that of bringing the sacred into a specific relation with the profane in such a way that Christianity will not be contaminated but communicated, and that modern society will not be deformed but sanctified.

Questions for Discussion

1. What aspect of work is this chapter chiefly concerned with? What tension does the Christian feel in confronting the world? What fundamental questions and facts does the author bring forward in this connection?
2. What are the inadequacies of some of the approaches to the problem of the Christian in his work and his relation to the world?
3. How can secularization be seen as a positive Christian value? Discuss. What is the Christian's task here?
4. How does the Christian's faith in Christ make possible his acceptance of the world? Explain the statement that "only the Christian is the truly 'worldly' man." What are four advantages of an approach which finds positive Christian value in the secularization process?
5. How can the relation of work to the future and to the beyond be distinguished? Why is it especially important today to recognize the value of the present in man's approach to work?

XIII
THEOLOGY AND WORK:
CONCLUSION

In an attempt to find a method of continual reevaluation of the work of the Christian or at least to develop a fundamental attitude toward the reassessment of the meaning of work in the Christian life, the survey of work in this collection of essays seems to bring us to the following conclusions.

A Contemporary Synthesis

First, *it is up to the Christian today to learn the meaning of work for today, to integrate his citizenship in the two cities, the human and the divine, in which he presently finds himself.*

Almost every selection in our anthology points to a need for an up-to-date re-evaluation of the human meaning of work. What this means for a theology of work is this: The radical changes in family structure pointed out by the sociologists, the growing "importance" of the child, the emancipation of woman, the personality crisis faced by a revolutionary large-size community of retired workers — each of these changes forces the theologian to reinterpret the meaning of work in the lives of each of the members of the Christian family. Furthermore, the ethical problems presented by automation, technology, and business' employment of psychocultural techniques on employees tell the theologian that work is no longer simply a question of an individual or small group of men confronting nature and using materials, but has become a complicated phenomenon where economy and society and international well-being are continually and intimately involved with a nation of workers.

Our changing world impresses upon us the importance of the

present. Tomorrow will demand its own re-evaluation of the factors involved in work and a deeper search for new meanings from the future findings of the sciences and arts.

Loss of Religious Character

A second conclusion is that *work in our historical secularistic context has lost its religious characteristic.*

This is perhaps the outstanding problem presented in the selection "Toward a Theological Meaning for the Daily Work of Christians": How can we explain the Christian's attitude toward the passionate attraction which he spontaneously feels for the earth and human progress? How can we account for his ability to see human activity as human, to experience the material world as material, as nondivine, and his inability in most cases to live his life in an atmosphere where God is present, where he might sense the supernatural nature of his acts?

Despite the *fact* that the Christian's work is connected with the kingdom of God, the *sense* of vocation in work has practically speaking disappeared. On the other hand, it is no longer satisfying or sufficient to interpret work simply as man's labor-payment to society. Work today is coming to refer to man's full use of his potential to materially benefit his fellowmen and to achieve his own self-fulfillment.

In his chapter on "Work and Play in the Secular City," Harvey Cox points out how urbanization and secularization have basically altered work and its meaning for us. These two tendencies have emancipated work "from the religious character it has retained from the period when it was interpreted as a spiritual experience." However, if secularization brings problems along with it — and it does — Cox is much more concerned to be positive, to show the possibilities presented by secularization. It is a "rather dangerous liberation," but at the same time makes it possible for man "to increase the range of his freedom and responsibility and thus to deepen his maturation." Christian man is being asked to plunge deeper into secularity than he has ever dared before. Work, then, has become a much more positive and powerful force in human life than ever before.

Positive Valuation of Leisure

A third conclusion is that *leisure too is destined to receive a strongly positive definition.*

Paula Zelipsky presented very clearly the challenge of leisure in the life of the aged, those who are "beyond work." Norris Clarke showed that more and more of everyone's life will come under the heading of leisure. What to do with leisure time is a deep problem on the human level. What then is the meaning of this radical change of a daily life schedule in terms of the Christian commitment? It seems that theologians must necessarily learn to discover positive Christian values and meanings for leisure. As long as work was considered in the context of labor-payment, work remained more or less the opposite of leisure. Work is now coming to be defined as the full utilization of an individual's potential for material benefits and personality development through productive self-expression. In a similar way, leisure now takes its stand right next to work, complementing it by using man's potential for providing more complete cultural, social and psychological benefits for himself and others. Perhaps, Cox suggests, only after we have sufficiently secularized our notion of work can we begin to correctly realize to what God is calling us:

> The call which comes to man from the bible, the *vocatio,* summons him not to a job, but to joy and gratitude in whatever he is doing. It is equally relevant at work and at play — or in the "new leisure" in which work can become endowed with the quality of play.

Leisure is coming to be a most important factor in man's life. Leisure demands a deeper significance than that of being a game or a rest period from work. In many ways, this book bespeaks the need for a theology of leisure.

Drive toward Integration

The fourth conclusion we can draw from the survey of work in the social sciences is that *there is a strong general tendency toward the integration of all human activity, personal and productive.*

Cultural anthropologists such as Cora Du Bois attempt to find

the roots and directions of the behavioral customs which characterize a nation, in order to connect what seem to be disparate patterns
of activity. On a much more pragmatic level, as was pointed out
in A. G. Brown's article, the organization in its employment of
the social psychologist revels in the discovery of the interrelation
between the personal and productive dimensions in the lives of the
individuals and groups whom they hire.

In these pages there has been no attempt to confine in any way
the meaning or definition of work. Perhaps one could make the
accusation that the concept of work in this survey was left entirely too vague, signifying nothing more specific than productive
human effort. However, it was only in this freedom to allow the
broadest definition of work to appear that the challenge which
secularity brings forth becomes clear: the challenge to man to
integrate all the facets of human existence, personal and community life, manual and mental effort, affective and reflective experience.

Beyond the attempt to *integrate* the aspects of human life into
a unity, we have become more and more aware through the advances of the socio-psychological sciences of the possibilities for
further *development* of human life on earth. Man is coming to
realize, for example, how radically he belongs to this world. Independent of his consciousness or rationality, man through his
body — his body *as subject* — is sensitive to the world and in
dialogue with the world. Merleau-Ponty would maintain that man
remains a body-subject in this sense of unconscious and irrational
communication with the universe around him even in the highest
accomplishments of his spirit. Everything on earth lends itself to
a relationship of dialogue with man, especially as things approach
the level of spirit and person. Man longs to cultivate and develop
this communication with all levels of existence in the world. This
desire is most clearly seen among the architects, artists, musicians,
writers, and what we might call the "creative" scientists and inventors.

Knowledge and Creativity as Factors

A fifth conclusion we can draw from our study is *the importance
of knowledge and creativity in the world of work* — creativity in

all its forms, in man's increasing discovery of himself especially in his relationships to other men and in his inventive improvement of the technological control he exerts upon nature. In this country in the last fifty years we have tripled the gross national product, we have increased threefold the amount of goods and services available to every man, woman and child. The quality of our civilization which explains this marvelous record is technology, man's ever-growing control of the powers hidden until now in the universe. This accomplishment is not due to a higher proportion of workers or longer hours of labor; the achievement is a result of the technological improvements which have provided a large increase in the output per man hour in our nation. Hence, we are not surprised to hear Professor Herbert A. Simon of the Carnegie Institute of Technology develop the thesis that "the bulk of the productive wealth of our economy is not embodied in factories and machines but is to be found in the knowledge and skills stored in men's minds." We see large corporations devoting mountains of money and the best minds they can find to *research*. The men in big business place a premium on *creativity,* as is clear from Helen Rowan's article in *Think* magazine, a revolutionary new kind of aesthetic where the artists are resculpturing the entire city of man. For in a highly developed economy like ours, progress depends primarily upon the accumulation of knowledge and skill and only secondarily upon the accumulation of physical wealth. If the quantity and quality of technical accomplishments have skyrocketed in the past few decades, we can be sure that the store of knowledge is going to increase in quantity and quality even more rapidly than it ever has in the past.

James W. Trent and his associates focus on the variables which influence an individual in his choice of life-goals; this kind of selection usually occurs during the formal education process. Such goals become a dominant consideration for life itself and consequently a theology of work must take such life-goals and the motivation behind them into account.

Revolutionary Advances

The sixth conclusion concerns *the revolutionary character of humanity's creative advances.* It seems to be a commonplace to claim that man and creation are becoming more and more unified. This degree of communion has taken a long time, much effort and many mistakes to achieve.

To more graphically illustrate the stages in man's dialogue with nature, Eric Hoffer in an article, "Automation Is Here To Liberate Us" (*New York Times,* Oct. 24, 1965), retold the creation story of Genesis in terms of automation. When God created the world, he automated it and there was nothing left for him to do. When, however, God made man to his image, it was natural that man would try to emulate his creator, to become a creator, to create a man-made world that would know, control and employ what God had created, and ultimately to automate (or re-automate) the world as man wants it. Man began slowly; but he deserved blue ribbons for inventions such as fire, the wheel, the sail, the plow, language and writing. The machine age proved that man was really growing up. "The machine was man's way of breathing will and thought into inanimate matter." This, however, was nowhere near the goal of complete automation, because many men, women, and children had to become parts of the steel and steam machines in order to make them work. But then, almost unnoticed, the automated machine appeared as a result of mathematicians and engineers trying to duplicate the human brain. This not only freed man from the toil and drudgery of work but *eliminated* him from the productive process. Cybernation began when a machine system was controlled and guided by a computing machine. Cybernation by its very nature eliminates the need for human labor. Man is on the threshold of an automated world, where it seems he will, like God on the seventh day, have nothing to do but rest.

The story makes us smile. But it does make us aware that we live in a world in which work finally appears in all its power, personal and communal, metaphysical and historical. We have come to acknowledge the power of matter. We have come to the point, says M.-D. Chenu in his *Theology of Work,* where man realizes that "scientifically and intelligently, his destiny is also achieved in matter, since his power and mission enable him to humanize it by his work, and so to accomplish the synthesis of man and nature" (p. 29).

Context—The World

The seventh conclusion is that *work must be looked at today in the context of the whole world.* In many ways technology has brought about the awareness of the unity of the entire human family. There is a world community of scientists cooperating in research. Corporations today think, plan and organize their efforts in terms of the world and space. The latest booklet describing the activities of the Ford Foundation is entitled *Context — the World.* The Church also has shown her concern over the world community and world government in the Vatican II constitution on the Church in the Modern World.

On the point of the solidarity of man and the casting aside of national boundaries and prejudices, the scientific and theological worlds are already in agreement. Joseph Thomas is quick to recognize the collective and global viewpoint of productive labor and the insights afforded by a survey of the movement of man's increasing control over nature. In his vision of the meaning of work in God's plan he sees that "the completion of humanity and of the universe will also be the final and total manifestation of the riches of God" and "the fraternal community of all men in Christ will be the perfect manifestation of the mystery of the Love which is in God and which is God himself."

Man and Work

Work today finds itself at the center of human existence and consequently also at the heart of Christian existence. Work is not the essence or totality of life as Marx would have us believe. Neither is work peripheral to, or a precondition for, some authentic kind of human existence found only in contemplation, in freedom from work.

Labor is a true form of human life and becoming. History is founded on human effort. Work is the activity by which man projects around himself a human milieu, says Merleau-Ponty, and transcends what nature gives to his life. Civilization is the shape of man's creative openness, the mode of man's mastery of himself and the world about him, the declaration of his independence of matter, the expression of his superiority over it.

To those who would prefer to define contemporary man as a

contemplative rather than a worker, Chenu comments: "The activity of work is still the normal vehicle for man's perfection or his undoing. It is a means by which he can express himself and the only means, unfortunately, in which the mass of humanity can find self-realization." In humanizing the universe man humanizes himself. Work for us today is a way to become man.

Today a new overall image of man is emerging. We have seen from a survey of the meaning of work in the social sciences, for example, the changing structure and function of the human family, the problem of educating the child for a work career and the crisis of the retired worker in a world revolutionized by automation, the totally new demands on the human sources of creativity which face the expanding corporations, the artist as well as the ordinary worker who can expect a growing number of leisure hours in the coming years in which he must become himself. We have tried to show how this new man makes theological reflections and approaches the meaning of work in the life of the contemporary Christian. For this new man, seen through the eyes of Christian faith, is born from the grace of God. This grace is at work in all human work helping to build the kingdom of God. A theological reflection upon the insights of the social scientists, like that of Joseph Thomas, allows the Christian in the secular world to discover in "the image of Christ the possibility of a love which gives to work and toil a value in time and eternity." Johannes B. Metz further argues that the theologian must learn to look for positive Christian values in the process of secularization, since "the secularization of the world is not unambiguously the world's protesting rejection of God's acceptance of it, but also primarily the historical manifestation of its acceptance by God." The work of God still continues (John 5:17) and is accomplished principally in the human person in his openness to the kingdoms of God and man. But it is not only through man's *work* that the kingdom of God or the kingdom of man is achieved, for work is not the totality of man's activity. Man does not find in his daily work his complete meaning in relation to his fellowmen and God.

Man and Life

Life is of its nature self-expressive. On whatever level it exists life affirms itself in whatever way it can. The life of man is personal life; the primary form of self-expression of personal life is the act of loving. Man also confronts and uses the material world productively; the primary form of self-expression of man's productive life is the act of working. Loving and working are both in their deepest meaning creative and consequently self-transcending. As a social being, man also lives a life of community. The human community is also self-expressive in its communal life and productive life through loving and working.

Just as Christians look to God as the model and meaning of life and love, they may likewise look to him as the model and meaning of their productive life. For, insofar as man is maker he images God the creator, not in creating something out of nothing but in the production of something somehow *new*. We should note that in our technological age man does far more than simply remold the raw material of nature; his products are on a far higher level than this and deserve to be called "creative." Neither should we forget that God is the creator-worker preeminent. And if we are made in the image of God, we should not anthropomorphize the work of God, but try in our work both as individuals and in the human community to approach the most creative self-expression of which we are capable.

The implication here is this: in his *living* God has unified his *loving* and *working*. His acts and deeds on men's behalf in history proceed from his love for men and are at the same time an expression of this love. Hence the ideal for each Christian is to unify love and work in his own life. One works out of love: a love for his own life, welfare, family, accomplishments, all within the love of God. One's love also grows from his work: exhilaration and joy in the expended effort of body and mind for the service of man and God.

In this unification of loving and working in the Christian's life we see reflected the general tendency, as pointed out in the fourth conclusion of our study, toward the integration of all human activity, both personal and productive. In this light, too, we can see an ideal concept of work emerging which comprehends both a human and a specifically Christian meaning, namely, *humanly creative productive self-expression done out of love*. Most naturally then, one of the fruits of work is an increase in love and the ability to love. Thus, just as one grows in the ability to love, one learns more deeply the true meaning of work and the freedom which it brings. The unification of these two phases of human self-expression in a person's life needs time and experience. Moreover, the unity of love and work is not to be sought primarily in the individual event or in the single workday, but should rather be envisioned as the goal of a whole life's human endeavor.

The Challenge

Here, then, is the challenge which faces the Christian as he confronts material creation: to discover its meaning, purpose, direction, identity. Throughout these pages we have presented in a rather attractive light the discoveries of the meanings of work for individuals and mankind as a whole, which came to us through the research of the social scientists. There is also a darker side of today's world of work. In addition to the poverty and unemployment and unethical practices which abound in the business world, there are other difficulties brought about by the rise of technology and automation. For, if technology has been a liberator of mankind, it is also a demanding ruler. It forces today's man to live on a level of *abstraction* which no one before this century thought possible. It has made possible and almost necessary a life lived on the level of *externalization,* a second-hand life. Secular technology further demands *organization, standardization, impersonalization*—all of which are summed up somewhat pejoratively in the word "secularization." If science has transformed our planet and annihilated space, it has also left man without roots. Modern man faces himself as a stranger. The human person who tries to realize his uniqueness on a diet of externals will soon dwindle to a shadow.

In short, because secularization has both good and bad effects, it presents Christians and the Church with problems. One of the foremost of these, as we have seen, is the problem of the Christian and the meaning of the created world and his work in it. One of the most welcome results of Vatican II is that Christians are invited to try new methods, to experiment with new approaches to the solutions of their problems, that Christians are given in a formal setting the privilege of making mistakes and trying again.

We have tried in these pages to experiment with a rather new method of approaching one of the problems of Christian living. We presented some of the meanings of human work as seen by the sociologist, anthropologist, economist and educator and discovered in the insights of these social scientists material with which to make a fresh approach and fuller reflection on the problem of the Christian and his work.

Within this experiment, however, the Christian must ever keep fundamentally in mind that—even if he must be open to change, even if he must preserve a readiness to re-evaluate as well as an adaptibility to the demands of evolution—as a Christian he can still never forget that his "posture before the present" is love. The Christian affirms that "love is the most universal, formidable and mysterious of cosmic energies," says William Hamilton in "A Theology for Modern Man." But for the Christian love does not derive its content from the present world. "Its content and shape," continues Hamilton, "come from the reality we have grasped by faith, from the character of God given to us in the cross of Christ." We love, because, through faith, we have received God's love. Just as the direction of love comes from faith, love points forward and gives form and content to our hope.

In a Christian spirituality which encompasses the meaning of work, the reconciliation of attitudes which embrace not only the *individual* and the *community* but the *world made complex and diverse and yet one* through the work of mankind in this historical path from "tribe to technopolis" is one of the crucial Christian problems of our century. Herein lies the grand work for Christian intellect and heart: The progressive unification of our planet presumes intelligent dialogue between individuals and peoples, a willingness to learn from one another, a willingness to give our efforts to one another, a willingness to share each insight into the human spirit, whether it emerges from the quiet reflection of the theologian or is collated in the statistical tables of the scientist. For modern Christian man, work in the broad sense of the term is no longer the lot of slaves, nor the punishment of sin, but as Hamilton reminds us, "the expression of the very essence of man, the foundation of human solidarity in history and before history."

Questions for Discussion

1. What seven general conclusions are drawn from the survey of material in the preceding chapters?
2. How do the various conclusions relate to various themes in the earlier chapters?
3. Why is work at the center of human existence?
4. What is the relationship between love and work in the life of man? What bearing does the tendency toward integration have on this relationship? What ideal concept of work emerges here?
5. What challenge faces the Christian as he confronts creation? What posture should mark his attitude toward the present? Why? In this context, how does the Christian see the world of work?

Additional Readings

In addition to the references identified in the text and notes, the reader may find the following helpful in pursuing his study of various aspects of the problem of the Christian and his work.

On work and the family:

Claude Levi-Strauss, "The Family," *Man, Culture and Society,* Harry L. Shapiro, ed. (New York: Oxford, 1960).

Robert and Rhona Rapaport, "Work and Family in Contemporary Society," *American Sociological Review* 30 (June 1965), pp. 381-94.

Robert D. Strom, "The School Dropout and the Family," *School and Society* 92 (April 18, 1964), pp. 191-92.

On work and the aged:

Eugene A. Friedman, Robert J. Havighurst, *et al., The Meaning of Work and Retirement* (Chicago: University of Chicago, 1954).

Justus J. Schifferes, *The Older People in Your Life* (New York: Perma-book, 1962).

On the worker and his education:

Alexander W. Astin, "Identification, Motivation, and Training of Talented Students," *School and Society* 92 (April 18, 1964), pp. 186-89.

John W. Donohue, S.J., *Work and Education: The Role of Technical Culture in Some Distinctive Theories of Humanism* (Chicago: Loyola University Press, 1959).

Frederick Herzberg, Bernard Mausner, Barbara Bloch Snyderman, *The Motivation to Work* (New York: Wiley, 1959).

G. R. Kaback, "Automation, Work and Leisure: Implications for Elementary Education," *Vocational Guidance Quarterly* 13 (Spring 1965), pp. 202-6.

Harold L. Wilensky, "Work Careers and Social Integration," *International Social Science Journal* 12 (1960), pp. 543-60. Also in *Comparative Social Problems,* S. N. Eisenstadt, ed. (New York: Free Press, 1964).

On the worker and his culture:

Wilbert E. Moore, *The Impact of Industry* (Englewood Cliffs, N.J.: Prentice-Hall, 1965).

Clinton Rossiter, *Marxism: The View From America* (New York: Harcourt, 1960). Cf. esp. "Marxist Man," pp. 63-92.

Harry L. Shapiro, ed., *Man, Culture, and Society* (New York: Oxford, 1960), cf. articles by Ruth Benedict, E. A. Hoebel, G. P. Murdock and Robert Redfield.

V. H. Vroom, *Work and Motivation* (New York: Wiley, 1964).

On the worker and the organization:

Social Psychology (personality and organization):

Chris Argyris, *Integrating the Individual and the Organization* (New York: Wiley, 1964).

Burleigh B. Gardner and David G. Moore, *Human Relations in Industry*, 4th ed. (Homewood, Ill.: Irwin, 1964). This is a classic in this area.

Haire Mason, *Psychology in Management*, 2nd ed. (New York: McGraw-Hill, 1964).

Robert K. Merton, *Social Theory and Social Structure* (Glencoe: Free Press, 1957). Cf. esp. "Bureaucratic Structure and Personality," pp. 195-206.

Psychology (mental health of the worker):

Arthur Kornhauser and Otto M. Reid, *Mental Health of the Industrial Worker* (New York: Wiley, 1965).

Harry Levinson, *Emotional Health in the World of Work* (New York: Harper, 1964).

Ozzie G. Simmons and Helen McGill Hughes, *Work and Mental Illness: Eight Case Studies* (New York: Wiley, 1965).

On work and economic man:

George H. Dunne, S.J., ed., *Poverty in Plenty* (New York: Kenedy, 1964).

John Kenneth Galbraith, *The Affluent Society* (New York: Mentor, 1958). Cf. esp. chapters 1, 24, 25.

Francis X. Quinn, S.J., ed., *The Ethical Aftermath of Automation* (Westminster, Md.: Newman, 1962).

Robert Theobald, *Free Men and Free Markets* (Garden City, N.Y.: Doubleday-Anchor, 1965).

On work and the creative person:

Nathan A. Scott, Jr., ed., *The New Orpheus: Essays Toward a Christian Poetic* (New York: Sheed and Ward, 1964). See especially articles in Part I: "The Problem of Christian Aesthetic," and Part II: "The Nature of the Christian Vision."

Rose Slivka, "The Object: Function, Craft, and Art," *Craft Horizons* 25 (Sept./Oct. 1965), pp. 10-11.

Paul A. Witty, "The Gifted and the Creative Student," *School and Society* 92 (April 18, 1964), pp. 183-85.

On work and human leisure:

John Kenneth Galbraith, *The Affluent Society* (New York: Mentor, 1958). Cf. "Labor, Leisure and the New Class," pp. 259-69.

Philip H. Phenix, *Education and the Common Good* (New York: Harper, 1962). Cf. esp. "Recreation," pp. 107-118.

On the philosophy of work:

Although there appears no chapter on the philosophy of work as such in this anthology, the importance of a reflective approach to man and his work should be acknowledged. For those who wish to place work in a philosophic setting, the following readings are mentioned.

Remy C. Kwant, *The Philosophy of Labor* (Pittsburgh: Duquesne University Press, 1964).

Jean Lacroix, "The Concept of Work," *Cross Currents* 4 (1953), 236-50.

William F. Lynch, S.J., *Christ and Apollo* (New York: Mentor-Omega, 1960).

On the theology of work:

M.-D. Chenu, O.P., *The Theology of Work: An Exploration,* trans. by Lilia Soiron (Dublin: Gill, 1963).

Thomas E. Clarke, S.J., "The World Is Already Christic," *America* (May 29, 1965), pp. 800-03.

Simon Doniger, ed., *The Nature of Man in Theological and Psychological Perspective* (New York: Harper, 1962). Cf. esp. William Hamilton's "A Theology for Modern Man."

Donald W. Reck, S.J., "A Theology of Work," *Catholic Mind* 64 (February 1966), pp. 40-48.

Peter Schoonenberg, S.J., *God's World in the Making* (Pittsburgh: Duquesne University Press, 1964), esp. pp. 135-84.

Pierre Teilhard de Chardin, S.J., *Building the Earth* (Wilkes-Barre, Pa.: Dimension Books, 1965).

Marcel van Caster, S.J., "Human and Christian Meaning of Work," *Lumen Vitae* 20 (1965), pp. 283-306.

INDEX